C000104141

Stuff Aspergers Like

A Humorous View of Asperger's Syndrome

J.F. Browne

Copyright © 2018 by J.F. Browne.
All rights reserved.

ISBN: 978-1-7923-0102-5

Cover Image: Eakkaraj Boonrod | Dreamstime.com

Contents

IV. Thoughts and Their Processes

V. Hobbies/Special Interests/Leisure Activities

VI. Education and Learning

I.

Socialization, Conversation and Communication

Staring Contests—Winning and Losing

Aspergers often get caught in sticky situations when it comes to making eye contact in social settings. Specifically, they usually don't make any eye contact, or they stare too hard and too long. It's really a damned if they do and damned if they don't situation and there are too many conflicting messages when it comes to mastering this skill the neurotypicals do with ease.

Don't stare at someone you're attracted to too long. In other words, don't stare at something you want.

Do make eye contact during interviews. So, stare when you want something?

Hold her gaze in a moment of romance to let her know you're into her.

Don't hold her gaze too long when you first meet her at the gas station, because she'll think you're a weirdo.

Some researchers have said that all men, to some degree, have a form of autism, or what may be called an extreme left-brain.

This must be why most men, confused by the algorithm of staring, have no choice but to stare at a woman's breasts.

Think about it.

The eyes have become a source of repeated punishment and stress. After countless attempts to succeed in making the right amount of eye contact and failing through no fault of their own, men have given up.

The breasts provide a safe, neutral area to focus on while attempting to have a conversation. Unlike eyes, breasts won't roll when they're exasperated with you. They don't squint to make evil faces when you've done something wrong. And breasts never catch a man looking at another woman.

Such a shame.

Normally, Aspergers can explain their behaviors in a logical way so that others don't judge or misunderstand them. Phrases like, "I'm sorry if I'm not making eye contact. Sometimes I have to look away from someone to concentrate or stay focused," would almost guarantee forgiveness on the neurotypical's behalf.

But sadly, "I'm not trying to look at your breasts. The Asperger in me made me do it," is likely to leave the Asperger (male) with a couple of black eyes, rendering him unable to practice his eye contact skills and start the same, self-blaming pathway all over again.

Don't Stand So Close to Me

An encounter with an Asperger may have prompted Sting to sing his famous song, "Don't Stand So Close to Me." Aspies are known for not being good judges of personal space. If there's no one else in the elevator but you and the Aspie, her distance to you may seem like at least 100 people are trying to pack in.

Over time, Aspergers will learn to judge personal space, especially with the help of cues provided by those PhD Aspergers who spend every waking moment studying their special interest of themselves. But a word of caution: Instructions such as "Stand an arm's distance away" leaves the gate open to a flood of discussion since this is clearly a subjective concept. After all, every arm length is different. Should he use his arm length? The other person's? Is there an average arm length value he should use for reference? Despite the potential for confusion, unless the Asperger reaches out, grabs the other person's arm and places it on himself in an inappropriate area, this social situation is one that won't get out of hand.

A human being has the potential to emit dozens of scents. Because scents are stimuli Aspies are sensitive to, one would think the Aspie would want nothing more than to stay as far away as possible. But for some, neither shampoo, nor body lotion, nor perfume, nor aftershave is likely to make the Aspie take even a few steps away. Okay, maybe if ALL THREE of these are REALLY, REALLY strong. Then they're guaranteed to stand at least two city blocks away.

Being Asperger Snobs

Those who say Aspergers don't like socializing couldn't be more wrong. Aspies love socializing, especially with their own kind. Essentially, Aspergers are Asperger snobs.

The preference for another Asperger's company may not be stated explicitly. Imagine the lawsuits that would launch over a classified ad for a roommate with the caveat: No neurotypicals please. Okay, so not many lawsuits would be launched. However, the Asperger may state preferences with sentences like, "I like people who conversate like me," "It's easier to talk to some people," or, "I like those like me."

This snobbery starts early in life and is even encouraged by professionals and parents. The parent is advised to start exposing the child to other children with Asperger's, or at least other children who share their special interests because if not, quality opportunities in communication will be lost.

As adults, these Aspergers take solace in their own kind by seeking out memberships to groups with interests like sci-fi, strange sounding bugs normal people can't pronounce and dressing up in even stranger outfits on any given day but Halloween. They can also seek higher education where they're more likely to find dozens of people who enjoy reading the same set of books by the authors they've researched for years as adolescents. And in the workforce, an Aspie's special interest, such as computers or laboratories, naturally land them among similar company.

Last but not least, there are Internet forums to chat with other Aspergers and even dating sites for those interested in shagging, or, uh, "snagging" someone who not only looks good, but is mentally wired in all the good ways as well.

After so much pampering in the form of being able to hang out with their own kind, is it any wonder some of them get mad when forced to be in a setting that requires they talk to people who don't care about the annual ratio of discovered to extinct species?

Conversation with Purpose

If you have something important to say, say it. If you have something meaningless to say about your weekend, the new co-worker down the hall, the reality TV show featuring the slutty women in the town or anything else that doesn't require an answer to get something done or solve a problem, don't say anything to an Aspie.

Most people talk to share experiences and bond with their fellow man or woman. An Aspie prefers having a conversation with a purpose, or to convey something meaningful, such as something needed to make a decision. Some hate small talk and chit-chat and see very little point in sitting around on a lazy weekend afternoon rambling. Unless they're rambling about their special interest. Then, small talk can go on for days.

Since most neurotypicals enjoy small talk (as well as closeted Aspergers pretending to be neurotypicals), this may be a source of frustration for friends, co-workers, spouses and families.

Judy would rather not gossip about the *American Idol* results. Even if it *is* considered "employee bonding" that you are paid to do instead of transferring client files to different folders.

John may not get why his wife insists on having heart to heart conversations about their feelings and interests. After all, they aren't prepping for an episode of *The Newlywed Game*, where they must remember each and every detail about each other to win the big dollar prize.

There is no point in asking everyone at the employee meeting how they're doing. Given previous employee meetings, the answer will likely consist of putting a chipper, fake smile on their faces and responding, "great," even though it's 6:00 a.m., they fear getting laid off and a daily diet of what's served in the employee cafeteria has left them regularly constipated.

It's best to get right down to the minutes.

Monologues

History has a way of giving credit or too much credit to one person who doesn't deserve it.

Those who experienced the pleasure or pain of high school literature may have been falsely told that Shakespeare was the great creator of monologues. Like many other exaggerated parts of history, that simply is not true.

Hamlet had nothing on the Asperger.

When Aspergers are interested in having a conversation, they aren't interested in having a conversation *with* you. They're interested in performing a conversation *for* you—a performance that demonstrates their knowledge or expertise in a given area.

Get an Asperger excited about a particular topic during a conversation and everyone else involved in the conversation may as well exit stage left.

"Do you take supplements?" will be the Asperger's innocent opening line, giving the allusion you're about to have a conversation that requires more than one person. "I'm surprised so many people are taking multivitamins these days that don't have much glutathione in them. Out of all the supplements that are going to save us from getting cancers and other diseases, it's going to be glutathione. If everyone were taking their glutathione, we wouldn't have nearly half as many diseases that are caused by cells not repairing themselves or conditions that occur when the body is exposed to free radicals. Sure, it's not an essential amino acid and the body can synthesize it on its own from L-cysteine, L-glutamic acid and glycine, but obviously when you look at all the incidences of diseases, it's clear our bodies aren't making enough of it. And it is so essential for so many processes in the human body, like the immune system, DNA synthesis, DNA repair, protein synthesis and enzyme activation."

No one else will be able to get a word in, offer insight, agree, disagree or even express that they're tired of having the conversation because the Asperger will continue without pause or intermission. This will happen until the curtain is closed, otherwise known as the other person walking away.

Borrowing Phrases

One speech characteristic you may find an Asperger using is a borrowed phrase, jargon or sentence structure they've seen or heard.

Although many Aspies have a love of language, sometimes it's easier (especially when trying to convey the right information to NTs) to use a stock phrase that's common or that has been used in other social situations to get the point across, especially if they've heard it many times before and know it's a socially acceptable way of speaking they may otherwise have a hard time construing on their own.

Essentially, like salespeople, Aspies have an extensive list of "upsells," "rebuttals" and other already scripted responses ready when they need it.

Some Aspergers like to use movie quotes.

Depending on the rating of the film and the social situation, this may or may not be a good idea. It could get the laugh of the party. Or a few choice four-letter words popular with Aspergers and NTs.

Below are some classic movie quotes an Asperger could use in various situations. Warning: If you're an Aspie, it isn't recommended you use most of these responses unless you're one of those Aspies skilled in some solo form of athletics like running amazingly fast.

Scenario: A 30-page paper that's due in 20 minutes disappears from your hard drive.

Movie: *10 Things I Hate About You*

Quote: "The shit hath hittith the fannith."

Said by David Krumholtz's character Michael Eckman after anything planned goes awry.

Scenario: Mother, father, friend or any random NT trying to force excessive socialization on the Aspie.

Movie: *Wayne's World* with Dana Carvey.

Quote: "[Insert name of person suggested to socialize with] is nobody's friend. If [insert name again] were an ice cream flavor, he'd be pralines and dick."

Carvey's character Garth Algar tries to convince someone a certain television producer isn't anyone's favorite.

Scenario: Trying to explain to the woman who wants you to cheat on your partner, you're not that type (remember the Asperger morals).

Movie*: Anchorman*

Quote: "You are a smelly pirate hooker. Why don't you go back to your home on Whore Island?"

Will Ferrell's character Ron Burgundy insults his female co-worker, Veronica Corningstone, portrayed by Christina Applegate. Not an effective way to speak to any female co-worker in the office setting, of course, but you must be careful this one doesn't escape after imbibing your favorite alcoholic beverage at the annual company party.

Being the Anthropologist

Add anthropologist to the list of potential careers for the Asperger.

This would be a natural role for her because she has already spent so many years practicing.

Since Aspergers don't pick up on the social rules neurotypicals follow intuitively, they must rely on their intellect to learn how to behave, please and avoid offending others. This is done by observing how people in the neurotypical culture act, taking good notes and trying to assimilate into the culture through imitation.

This works sometimes. Other times, being the anthropologist just functions as a good intellectual/entertaining activity for the Aspie as he takes notes on how the ugliest of toads well into their seventies manage to snag supermodels who moonlight as gold diggers.

As children, the rules of the neurotypical culture are quite simple. Defer to the adults in every situation. Raise hand before speaking in class. Don't interrupt others. Share. Etc. However, as an adult, the rules become quite different and often make little sense or change with levels of emotion, power possessed or the alcohol the neurotypicals consume during their social activities.

Which can make for some interesting notes in the laboratory journal. Take your social gathering for neurotypicals in their twenties. The most common setting for these gatherings occurs either at frat parties or overly priced rundown houses landlords get away with charging so much for because these neurotypicals receive endless financial support to cover these expenses. Most of these expenses are for beer, but a small portion of them are dedicated to tuition, fees and books.

The anthropologist Asperger notices there are several recurring types of drunks in the culture and is careful to memorize these profiles, so she may NOT imitate them.

There is the stripper drunk. Usually an attractive lady who's a member of the sorority holding the party. She associates alcohol with removing clothes as a way to please the gods, otherwise known as drunk males who will give her attention.

There is the angry drunk, often the boyfriend of the stripper drunk who becomes insanely jealous of the other gods she is pleasing and throws bottles, smashes things and results in the neurotypical party ending early.

The perspicacious Asperger realizes some neurotypicals must have really, really good deals with gods, because when they drink the holy alcohol, they are given special powers of transformation. During the week, they are anxious, socially awkward individuals. During the weekends, they metamorphose into people who tell jokes with ease and have no fear of grabbing someone in the areas growing up mom and dad taught were off limits due to being in the "bathing suit" region.

Punishing and Criticizing

Those into weird fetishes like S&M will enjoy being at the receiving end of an Asperger's commentary. She will give you the punishment you need by telling you exactly what the problem is and then some.

It isn't necessarily because they enjoy being sadists and humiliating people or crushing their hopes and dreams. Aspies are truly interested in the development and betterment of others.

Aspies really don't care who they're punishing or criticizing. Those of higher authority than them are not exempt and may even be the target. A teacher who makes a minor spelling mistake on a worksheet will be reminded of it during class. The same is true for a mispronunciation of a word, an explanation that distorts the truth or one that doesn't include a thorough answer.

As they grow older, Aspergers in relationships will turn to punishing their mates, leading to intense discussions over the way they maintain the house, raise the children and make financial decisions. Children bringing "A's" home may still be questioned if the test was not 100% correct, the Asperger parent asking which questions were missed, why those questions were missed and demand a speech on how the work that set the curve for the class could be improved even more.

If you're looking for a score of 100%, A+ or a perfect 10 from an Asperger, you won't find it. The best you can hope for is receiving Most Improved for making 5,000 errors because your competition made 5,001.

Controlling Playmates and Being Parents to Other Children

Parents who send their children to play with an Asperger child need not fret over the possibility of the lack of adult chaperones. The Asperger child will step up to the plate, boss the other children around, remind them of when they're being good and bad and structure the entire day of playtime to ensure the NT children are well supervised.

As children, Aspies were notorious for driving their playmates nuts because they treated them as subordinates versus equal play-mates. Before the doorbell rings, Asperger children may have al-ready drawn up an itinerary for the day, the first item on the agen-da being to conduct a long discussion—which is really a lecturing monologue—on the Asperger child's special interest of music hits of the '80s. This is also the music that will be played in the back-ground even if the other child hates the music or has expressed not wanting to hear any music at all.

If the Asperger child and the NT playmate happen to agree on what to play, there still will be conflict.

The Asperger child already has in mind how he'd like to play the game. He is unwilling to accept any suggestion as to how to build a structure other than the one he sketched when he woke up that morning and made a list of how he was going to play dictator building blocks with little Johnny.

Asperger children are great disciplinarians and will correct the other children and punish them when they get out of line. A sneeze will be quickly followed by a lecture on germs and sickness, with a trip to the sink to wash. This will occur while giving a lecture on the right way to scrub hands, how long to wash (recite the alphabet), the best soaps to use and why antibacterial soaps aren't good anymore because they increase bacterial resistance.

Just before the child leaves, he will be questioned about how he's doing in school. If he's doing poorly, he'll be castigated. If he's doing well, the Asperger child will ask his latest score on the test. If it was lower than his, the Asperger child will most definitely remind him of it.

With friends like these, who needs parents? Or teachers. Or public service announcements on how only you can prevent the spread of colds and flu.

J.F. Browne

Interrupting and C-ing Their Way into Conversation

One complaint that friends, family, partners, teachers and anybody who tries to have a conversation with an Asperger has is that they're frequently interrupted while talking.

Aspergers love to invite themselves to the conversation party. After arriving without an RSVP, they start commenting on topics without being asked. The *Boyz n the Hood* memorable quote, "This is a A-B conversation, you know, you can C your way out of it," could be the perfect retort for anyone having a conversation where the Asperger joins to offer some fact or piece of knowledge about the topic that no one asked for or wants to hear about.

When an NT is interrupted, there can be utter confusion when the interrupting statement from the Asperger isn't necessarily related to the current topic of conversation. For example, if the NT is talking about something the Asperger doesn't like, the conversation will quickly turn to something that does get the Aspie going. A statement from the NT about how she feels about the direction their relationship is going is not logically followed by one on the top cities that have done the best job of implementing bike lanes in the community. But it provides a fantastic way to get out of answering stupid questions about commitment and quality time.

If neurotypicals want to lessen this interruption, there is one easy solution: only talk about things the Asperger is interested in.

Aspies tend to interrupt when the conversation is boring to them, so picking things the Asperger enjoys will ensure you will never get offended by him cutting you off. The other upside to starting a conversation about the Asperger's interest is that you don't have to worry about being interrupted because he'll never give you a chance to say anything.

Different Sense of Humor

Some neurotypicals mistakenly think Aspergers don't have a sense of humor. The truth is, Asperger humor has a uniqueness that most neurotypicals don't always get. Either that, or they find it hard to see the humor because they're always the subject of it.

There are many ways to describe Aspie humor—dry, sarcastic, weird. But lack of humor—they're anything but. Let us examine a few examples.

Smarty-pants Humor

Usually best understood by people well-educated. The Asperger likes to tell these types of jokes because not only do they allow him to interact with people who are well-read and informed on historical and current events, it's also fun to confuse the people that aren't.

The Offensive Aspie

Hasn't quite mastered the art of knowing what's appropriate to joke about and what's not. He's often seen making jokes that are sexist, racist, too aggressive and just downright rude. Right before he's seen running in fear from the person who was clearly offended by the joke.

Dry Humor

Often elicited from Aspergers who are normally always mildly grumpy. They're probably cracking this joke during a setting that's making them even more grumpy, like a forced social gathering.

The Pun and Play on Words Guy

Loves to make humor out of regular conversation. Puns are even funnier when they allude to innuendo or junior high school humor, so to him, there's nothing more hilarious than purposely mispronouncing "publicist" as "pube-blicist" when referring to a sex scandal between a politician and their PR person.

Not Detecting Boredom

While most neurotypicals can easily tell if a person is bored or no longer interested in a conversational topic, this is a skill the Asperger often struggles with.

Simply announcing to the Aspie, "Let's talk about something else," or, "I'm bored," isn't likely to get the job done. No passionate, monologue-giving Asperger would take this suggestion at face value. Aspergers know that a bored neurotypical is simply a neurotypical who needs to be continuously given more information about the topic until an exciting part comes up to get them "in the mood."

When needing to exit a conversation from an Asperger caught up in the moment, one may be tempted to give a few gestures, both verbal and non-verbal, to give hints that they're bored or need to change topics. These gestures could include casually trying to change the subject, looking away from the person talking, yawning and suddenly finding the squirrel perched in the tree to be the most fascinating object of the century.

These tactics generally will not work with the Aspie when he or she continues to go on and on about some obscure topic that no one really cares about, like odd facts about Howard Hughes, and often more dramatic, aggressive approaches to escape the Aspie's lecture must be taken.

Like getting up and walking away while he or she is in mid-sentence.

Neurotypicals need not worry about being rude for "cutting off" the Asperger by leaving the conversation. If the Aspie is discussing one of his most passionate interests, he will most certainly finish his thoughts with or without you, continuing to talk until all 2,000 important points about the *Spruce Goose* have been made.

J.F. Browne

Long Pauses During Speech

There's an old saying that if you can't say something nice, don't say anything at all. For Aspies, this mantra should be if you have no clue what to say, just wait for a second before saying anything. Or a few seconds. Or a few minutes.

Because Aspergers reason through intellect and not intuition, they are used to analyzing each and every piece of conversation before figuring out what the correct response in each situation should be. If they've gotten their feet extremely wet in the social waters, Aspies have a stock full of responses to give, both verbal and non-verbal. However, if they happen to come across an unfamiliar social setting where they haven't watched a respected person give the proper response, they may draw a blank—leading to an exceptionally long delay before answering a question or making a statement.

The most obvious way to address this problem is to ask, "What do you mean by that?" or, "Give me a moment to answer." But things do get strange after saying that every couple of minutes or so. Some Aspergers either don't think to do this or don't want to. The next best thing is to launch into a great conversation about something they do understand.

That's right.

If you can't say something nice, always talk about the special interest.

The Social Delay
(Sequel to *The Social Network*)

It isn't always easy for an Asperger to detect the non-verbal and other parts of conversation that most neurotypicals can—tone, facial expressions, gestures, emphasis on certain words and innuendo. This doesn't mean some of them can't use these non-verbal parts of conversation and social interaction to determine what the other person is really trying to convey.

Some Aspergers will pick up on all these things, albeit minutes, hours and even days later after using their intellect to place the pieces together.

This could be called "the social delay."

The social delay involves the Aspie's uncanny ability to replay parts of the social interaction, piece by piece, from conversation to body language. While studying both the audio and visual components of this "film," the Aspie can sometimes detect what someone really meant. But unlike the box office hit *The Social Network*, the social delay usually doesn't involve multiple lawsuits at one of the film's leading characters after reviewing the sequence of events that happened and learning credit wasn't given where due.

The social delay could, however, lead the Aspie to overanalyze, interpreting things that aren't really there, especially if this film is replayed dozens and dozens of times. But most of the time it simply functions to clarify the things that are not readily available to the Aspie mind but easy as pie for the neurotypical to immediately figure out. Like the fact the annoying bartender at the restaurant probably wanted to ask you out. It wasn't obvious then, even though he was so close he was practically giving you mouth-to-mouth. He kept asking questions about you but seemed more interested in every body part on you BUT the part that was talking back to him. Days later after replaying this film, it became quite clear what his intentions were. This resulted in you actually contemplating a lawsuit in this film, as it was pretty obvious you never ordered a pat on the rear with your entree.

Keeping Quiet in Group Settings

Aspergers often like to keep quiet in groups, even if the groups are small.

The most obvious reason for an Aspie's reticence is he was dragged into this situation. C'mon! How many Aspies voluntarily join groups for chit-chat? If this is the case, the Aspie has probably entered into some kind of agreement with who is currently seen as the devil, but usually known as spouse, partner or friend, to attend some sort of uninteresting event and talk to even more uninteresting people to celebrate an occasion she doesn't officially recognize because she swore off holidays and birthdays a long time ago. These Aspies are great imitators and can force a smile and sound genuinely excited about your new baby, the house or your promotion.

They're not.

There's always the chance the Aspie really does want to partake in the conversation but is afraid of saying inappropriate things or interrupting. Often unable to get a feel for the rhythm of the conversation, the Aspie knows from past experience he tends to cut people off, tell a weird, off-color joke or make a comment that has nothing to do with the conversational topic. So, unless he's talking in a one-on-one setting, he keeps it tight-lipped. This guy truly wants to learn to socialize in a friendly manner, so give him the opportunity and forgive him if he flops.

He's trying.

Alternatively, an Asperger chooses to stay quiet because the topic of conversation does not interest her. It's a good bet there will be no small talk coming from her unless the topic changes to the special interest. Then, the Aspie will refrain from being quiet either for the rest of the group's gathering or until they—one by one—get up and leave because they are tired of listening to her.

And eventually everyone *will* leave.

Finally, a quiet Aspie is a well-trained Aspie. He is usually taught by the same person who, in the past, tried to drag him to various social events until he started to "act out" and make her pay for doing so. Or the lessons could have come from a therapist whose best advice was to "stay quiet" because she gave up trying to teach him neurotypical manners. This acting out included offensive jokes, interrupting, arguing, insulting, always talking about himself and ALWAYS, ALWAYS making the special interest the center of the conversation. Given the fact he hasn't said a word all night, it may be tempting to ask him what he's thinking.

Don't. He's been so good so far. You don't want to either break his success or make his trainer-wife bring the shock collar next time.

Acting

Every time an Asperger pretends to be excited about sharing a room with a dozen relatives they barely know during the holidays, they deserve an Academy Award. And like Hollywood, Aspergers who are forced to act at these social get-togethers too often will, ultimately, voluntarily put themselves in "rehab," consisting of locking themselves in their room, garage or den and doing nothing but absorbing themselves in their special interest for a while to get over people exhaustion.

Playing a character may be interpreted as the opposite of Aspies as their traditional left-brained thinking is thought of as being more right for the analytical environment versus the arts and the stage. But make no mistake about it, as they advance in life, Aspergers are expected to become excellent actors and often excel at it. From exhibiting a variety of animated expressions (surprised, shocked, concerned, excited) to adding the right scripted language based on the situation, an Asperger may play several roles that exhibit various tones, gestures and reactions within a 24-hour period.

Depending on the script, the Aspie can play roles and interact with other actors such as teachers, neighbors, parents, clerks, management, mailmen, etc. and insert all kinds of language to look normal. They can also conveniently employ the use of echoing the other actor's performance—smiling when someone else smiles, laughing after a laugh. Like a good actress, the Aspie studies her character before going into it by observing others.

For Aspies without the natural ability to put on an Oscar winning performance, many of those who've worked with them in a supporting actor role (as in counselor, therapist, researcher) recommend they take introductory acting and public speaking courses and workshops as a way to increase their ability to display the diverse emotional reactions that do not come naturally. Interestingly, renown actress Daryl Hannah (*Splash* and many others) was diagnosed as "borderline autistic" as a child.

Slang and the Urban Dictionary

Some Aspergers have a hard-enough time grasping the mysterious non-verbal and implied language of the neurotypical world. To make matters worse, there is the neurotypical world of slang they must master. Unlike the rest of the human verbal and non-verbal language, which only changes every so hundred years, the world of slang changes yearly, monthly and even weekly in some neurotypical environments like school. It also changes depending on the geographical location and the human's age. For these reasons and many, many more, it may be best the Asperger try to learn slang to decode neurotypical conversation but stay the hell away from using it in conversation.

Slang is an area that may best be left in the hands of a neurotypical friend to teach. The more socially knowledgeable NT friend can teach what is "in," "out" and what's likely to get you kicked out of an establishment if you say it aloud.

When the neurotypical friend is absent, there is an online, somewhat obscene version of *Webster's Dictionary* called Urban Dictionary at *urbandictionary.com*. Urban Dictionary contains all the current slang words and phrases you need to know but never use, especially around grandma. Started by a computer science major at California Polytechnic State University, the Urban Dictionary has millions of definitions and was even recognized by *Time* magazine as one of "50 Best Websites" of 2008. One of the very first slang terms defined was "the man," not someone with a Y chromosome, but someone who is "head of the establishment," put in place to "bring us down."

So, remember, boys and girls, use slang with caution. Many things other than the sky are "up." A "shortie" isn't an insult to your height, "well hung," doesn't mean the picture is placed on the best possible position on the wall and a "ho" won't necessarily provide you with good gardening tips.

Aspergerdar—Asperger Radar

Many members of a particular group have a method, albeit unconventional and sometimes labeled as stereotypical or "ist" way of spotting out another member of a group without having to even exchange words with them. Known as having the "dar," these groups have a particular list of items to check off or a particular algorithm to follow when assessing the person of interest before being the first to call it.

Some young Jewish adults will claim their Jewdar is more accurate than a sexy-voiced female GPS, especially when their radar picks up on a good-looking male/female who made up more than half of the Skokie, Illinois population in the '60s. Common traits included dark hair, a surname with "stein" or "berg" in it, a Jewish version of an afro—known as a Jewfro—bigger than any African-American wore even in the '70s and who otherwise showed no signs of piousness except excusing him or herself from college classes for the occasional religious holiday (not counting the weekly religious holidays whose services and rituals included drinking lots of something the Christians have nicknamed Jesus' blood).

A Northwestern University professor claimed to have scientifically shown that gaydar is real and that some people can, at a level greater than chance, point out Elton John quicker than most males can get their "rocket men" fired up while looking at naughty images.

Asperger radar is similar to other dars and being the observant, analytical, pattern-noticing people they are, some Aspergers have an Aspergerdar as accurate as the number of digits behind the decimal point in pi. The dar goes off like a test tornado alarm every week in the Midwest. If you're an Asperger or have a "friend" who is, you may have walked by a fellow Aspie and noticed a few things.

More than likely, you've spotted him in the same corner of the cafeteria, consuming the same disgusting sandwich he orders everyday (making stupid changes the chef cannot remember), wearing some hideous outfit he owns with a few variations (it's either a blue shirt, aqua shirt or navy blue shirt), and have been at the end of his monologues you weren't getting paid overtime to listen to, filled with facts only weirdos recite and cracking jokes that either no one understands or everyone is offended by.

You then thought, "Wow, I always order that same disgusting sandwich and make those stupid changes. I like wearing the same hideous pieces of clothing regularly. No one likes it when I swing by their cubicle to discuss species of weeds growing in the south. I think he's an Asperger like me. But I do make better jokes, though. And no one threatens to slap me when I do."

Responding to Stupid Shit People Say

In the world of viral web stuff, there have been a few memes going around that poke fun of others' ignorance. The "Stupid Shit People Say to/About [Insert Group or Popular Culture Topic]" are often hilarious and truthful. A "Stupid Shit People Say to Aspergers" could include a host of annoying things many neurotypicals say to an Aspie:

"But you're so intelligent."

"Isn't there a medication to take for that?"

"You don't really act friendly. Don't you like us?"

"What's going on in your head? You never fill me in."

"Will you help me with my computer?"

Perhaps one of the stupidest comments made to an Asperger who knows how to "blend" is that they simply do not have the disorder, blowing a major insult to the Aspie who has worked so hard to assimilate into NT culture.

An Asperger could take one of two approaches when answering these stupid questions. View the opportunity to educate and attempt to answer them seriously. Or just give the neurotypical a good, ASSperger answer that will run him off faster than...the mature recommendation is that you educate. But during those really bad days when you've had an interaction with one nuisance neurotypical too many, there are shortcuts to answering these questions. See the following examples:

"But you're so intelligent."–I agree. And it's not intelligent to assume someone with Asperger's isn't.

"Isn't there a medication to take for that?"—Yes. I heard big pharma is concocting some great formulas to help those with the disorder of constantly wanting to change other people. You'd probably tolerate them without side effects.

"You don't really act friendly. Don't you like us?"—Well, um... actually...no. I don't. Not at all.

"What's going on in your head? You never fill me in."—Mostly sexual fantasies about your friends. Your really attractive friends who admit they're attracted to me too. Want to know details?

"Will you help me with my computer?"—Yes, I will for free, but I will leave a code that allows me to hack in anytime afterwards.

Seriousness

The Asperger has the uncanny ability to maintain a serious composure. For that reason, you're likely to see him to look and act the same during both a funeral and a carnival.

Sometimes this is mistaken for being uptight. Sometimes it's taken as a lack of humor. But in reality, it's usually neither of those things, but a combination of several other things.

Aspies are known for taking things literally and not "reading between the lines." A conversation where both parties normally understand each other's implied meanings, metaphors and sarcastic comments normally elicits a variety of responses, laughter being one of them. The same conversation involving an Asperger talking to a neurotypical is likely to leave the Asperger with a WTF look and the neurotypical with a WTF is wrong with you look. The classic monotonous tone some Aspergers possess makes it a wiser choice they keep their day programming jobs instead of pursuing a career as a stand-up comedian.

Occasionally something said serious is taken as funny. That's because most neurotypicals find it all too weird to hear the details of the party you're planning for your pet fish. But you know the major decision of choosing between new, shiny rocks for the aquarium or giving them a treat of the expensive Flipper's Delight snack food is serious. Profoundly serious.

Aspergers play the role of serious so well, sometimes people will take them seriously when they are trying to be funny. It sometimes helps to laugh when you're telling the joke. But most of the time it doesn't. When reminded of the fact you're only joking, the frustrated neurotypical may respond with a statement like, "It's so hard to tell. It always sounds like you're being serious." To which you can reply in a serious manner, "I will try to work on letting you know when I'm just joking...seriously."

Going MIA at Social Gatherings

It's a misconception that Aspergers do not like to socialize. They do socialize—they just don't require nearly as much of it as neurotypicals do. When many Aspies either voluntarily agree to attend or are dragged by a leash to various social gatherings like birthday parties and reunions, they will spend a few minutes chatting before quickly moving on to something else that sparks their interest and is usually a solitary activity. This phenomenon is unofficially known as Going MIA at Social Gatherings.

The solitary activity may range from catching up on a work or personal project, reading the latest *JAMA: The Journal of the American Medical Association* to learn about the hottest news on statins or surfing the Internet. It's not that the Aspie is trying to be rude and shun everyone at the get-together—it's simply that they do not have a need to do any more socializing (unless everyone wants to have a discussion on how the greasy ingredients in the party dip fuel the demand for Lipitor). Pretending to do so will only result in boredom and irritation.

Neurotypical friends and family who don't understand the Asperger's reduced need for socialization may mistakenly coax or even demand the Asperger stop running away at these events and socialize more. They may make it a point to invite them to twice as many functions, thinking the Asperger simply needs "exposure" or "practice" in being more social. This can result in numerous reactive behaviors from the Asperger, ranging from creating excuses to being downright rude to guests because they feel they are forced into situations and words and feelings are being put into their mouths ("I don't have a social phobia...I am not shy...I just don't care for it.").

Eventually the Asperger gets smart and learns to use these "forced socialization" events to their advantage. They will agree to go to the friend's MBA party just because they know the friend has a NICE CD burner in the upstairs room where they can create a CD of the latest live Radiohead tunes. Or, they might think to themselves, "Oh, they own that cool dog. He'll be great to play with." Food is always a motivator for everyone, Asperger or neurotypical, and good grub may be worth a thousand small talks to some.

Flattery to the Intellect

The way to a man's heart may be his stomach, but the way to an Asperger's heart is through his head. That is, making it even bigger than it already is.

Although Aspergers may be socially awkward at times, they are damn smart individuals, many having above average intelligence and being more likely to hold degrees than the rest of the population. Although they know how brilliant they are, they are always interested in being told so repeatedly.

While most neurotypical people enjoy hearing how they make a person feel good, have warm personalities or are caring people, this does nothing for the Asperger. When trying to get in good with one, remember to always remind them of how much they know and preferably how much more they know compared to you. This can be important to remember when in a relationship with any Asperger. Greeting card companies might want to take note and design slogans for Asperger cards such as, "When you care enough to tell them they're the very best." Anniversary cards for neurotypical spouses might get the job done with, "You complete me in every way. For that, I am thankful." Anniversary cards for Asperger spouses should say, "You complete what I cannot do—and that is just about everything. For that, I am thankful."

When trying to complete a computer-related task—such as installing software, you might find yourself asking for help from someone in IT with poor manners and even poorer choice in clothing. By asking outright, you're more likely to get the response, "I can't believe he is so stupid he doesn't get [insert extremely complicated task for everyone except those that like to address their girlfriends in the bedroom with pet names like Susie Linux]."

There are much more efficient ways to approach the Asperger. Start off by approaching him or her and bringing up some random fact about computers and software. This will spark the Asperger's interest (you are talking about their probable special interest after all) and make him much more receptive. Then begin the butt kissing. Some phrases to try and experiment with are, "You are so much more educated about these things than I am," or, "I'm stupid, but I know you have the answer," or even, "You will be the next Bill Gates." You see the point by now. After you have complimented the Asperger a million times, he will be more than happy to assist you.

He probably will also give you other advice and facts you never asked for and turn a 30-second answer into a ½-hour lecture.

Speaking Factanese

Aspergers love facts and love to insert them into conversation. You might find yourself chatting with an Asperger and notice every other line is a fact or data supporting a fact. It is so integrated into the conversation, you wonder how on earth anyone could know so much, either about one specific or many disciplines. This phenomenon is known as Speaking Factanese.

Aspergers are born bilingual, the 1st language being their native, the 2nd being Factanese. It's not that Factanese can't be understood by the neurotypical. It's just darn hard to speak it with the same fluidity as the Asperger. To help you recognize Factanese and become more fluent, please study the following sample Factanese passages:

Conversation 1: The Father's Day Gift

Asperger: I can't decide what to get my father for Father's Day. He likes cookware.

Person A: Get him Mr. Cook's Oven Mitt.

Asperger: If I'm going to get an oven mitt, I'll get Mr. Manly Bakes instead. Mr. Manly Bakes withstands 500 degrees Fahrenheit of heat, while Mr. Cook's only withstands 450.

Conversation 2: The Microwave Popcorn Dilemma

Asperger: I'm going to pop some popcorn.

Person A: I stopped doing the microwave popcorn thing after I found out about the whole diacetyl and lung cancer link.

Asperger: Some companies have stopped using (emphasizes the correct pronunciation—which Person A didn't do) *diacetyl* flavoring. You should check out each company's website for their policy on it—or learn to make homemade popcorn.

Conversation 3: The Fiber Kick

Person A: I'm going to start getting more fiber in my diet because I want to be healthier.

Asperger: You should really consider what type of fiber you need more of. There are two types. Soluble lowers your cholesterol while insoluble helps you pass bowel movements better. (This conversation is taking place over dinner, by the way.)

After careful study, you may have spotted the facts inserted into each sample conversation—the temperature the oven mitt can withstand before burning father's hand, the fact potentially safer microwave popcorn brands exist and the type of fiber to seek out based on your personal needs—cholesterol lowering or easier defecation. By continuing to study these examples and looking for similar patterns in your everyday conversation with an Asperger, you too can become fluent in Factanese and find a way to insert obscure information about boats, weather and walrus genitals into any conversation.

Providing More Than the Minimum Coverage

Like other areas of life, in conversation, details are important for the Asperger. Even the details that aren't important to everyone else, weren't asked for and no one cares about. When asking the Asperger, a simple question, they're likely to give you more information than what's necessary, otherwise known as providing more than the minimum coverage.

More than the minimum coverage usually takes place in two categories: a Shakespearean monologue for a yes/no question and TMI—Too Much Information. TMI is, of course, not just extra conversation, but the kind of coverage that does not make for good dinner conversation. This will often take place in groups, such as a walk in the park on a hot summer day, for example.

Let's say the Asperger drank several bottles of water, but still hasn't had a need for a bathroom break like every other member in the group. "You probably are dehydrated," a fellow hiker may suggest.

"You're probably right," the Asperger replies. "In fact, I must be dehydrated because my urine was extremely dark this morning. And I've been terribly constipated as well. But it may be due to my bathroom rhythms. I have certain times of the day when I urinate and hardly ever go off schedule. It must not be time to urinate yet. But having bathroom schedules are convenient because you always know when you're going to go. Except of course, when it's time and you can't find a bathroom. There have been two times there wasn't a bathroom around and I am so glad I was wearing dark pants because..."

We can all see that the TMI checkpoint was missed long ago.

While other monologues may not hit the TMI scale, they still provide more than the minimum coverage. Directions to the pharmacy come with the history of why all the streets are named what they are named, the business that used to occupy the pharmacy building, the arrangements of the aisles and the order of medicines in them. Hopefully, she or he will remember the social rule of not asking what you're buying, but probably not, and if not, at least you'll be provided with several cheaper alternatives to Mr. Hooper's hemorrhoid cream.

Correcting

In the world of Aspergerness, there are usually two colors: black and white. It's either right or wrong, with no possibilities of shades in between. However, for many Aspergers, the color palette can be expanded slightly to allow for times when others forget what color an issue should fall under. That color is red—for correction.

Aspergers love to correct, both people and inanimate objects. It is an innate tendency that they attempt to conceal through numerous methods—biting the tongue or lip, pretending not to see or hear the mistake or maybe convincing themselves that there really is another way of looking at it. But sooner or later, a huge volcanic-like reaction will occur in their bodies and minds, forcing them to tell the world just how things really should be.

This is helpful at times. We'd all like to know when there's spinach on our teeth. If you hire an Asperger as your personal assistant, you ensure you'll never be in the presence of your future in-laws with an unzipped fly. Ditto for bad grammar, incorrect or twisted facts, mispronunciations and your tendency to stretch or leave out parts of a story. But other times, when most neurotypicals leave the red pen in the desk drawer, the Asperger opens a fresh pack in case one runs out of ink.

An otherwise romantic, tender moment between a couple can quickly turn sour by the Asperger's need to correct. "Your eyes are as blue as the sky," will quickly be followed by, "The sky is more cyan than regular blue. If you think my eyes are cyan, that's fine, but blue isn't the best descriptive word if you're going to be using the sky as a simile." This same partner was rebuked last week for writing a love letter rife with spelling errors that the Asperger circled in red and returned.

A lover who finds him or herself in this situation can be redeemed by the all-time symbol of couple apology and makeup: buying a gift for the Asperger partner. Red pens and correction fluid make good stocking stuffers as well as books containing titles like "Myths Uncovered," "Secrets Exposed" and "The Truth About," as they give the Asperger the reassurance that you agree upon the core values of any good relationship: trust, love and a strong sense of telling each other and the rest of the world how everything that comes out of their mouths or is written by their hand is completely screwed up.

Imitation

Aspergers will often imitate to get through various social situations when they are unsure of how to navigate them using their own social skills. This imitation may include social gestures, professional and business mannerisms, party talk or even entire characters, such as "The Girl Pretending to Laugh at the Stupid Boy's Jokes."

Years ago, there was a fast food commercial that aired in America which depicted a business man walking into the restaurant, spotting one of his co-workers and saying something like, "Oh, hi person at work I don't really know or care about and I'm just here to get my coffee," or something of that nature. There is no better explanation for the Asperger's need to imitate. Some situations call for very specific social behaviors and the Asperger must perform them on cue whether it feels natural or not.

In most cases, imitation is good. If you told the co-worker, "I was really hoping you'd call in today. I'm going to have to find another cafe, so I can avoid running into you," this unwelcoming attitude toward your colleagues would most certainly get back to the boss and your unemployment claims would outnumber breast implants in Hollywood.

But imitation can have a very dark side. Adolescent Aspergers who imitate "the bad kids" will not only find themselves in trouble at school but looking damn ridiculous as well. Imagine your coke-bottled glasses, pocket protector wearing, ant-farmed carrying kid grabbing his crotch (held up by suspenders) and telling the teacher, "I don't do homework #$%@*, I do your mom." Point taken?

Bad imitation is scary and even an adult Asperger can succumb to it. Adult Aspergers may find themselves imitating people they really don't like or admire, pretending to take on values they really don't have, faking emotions that are exactly the opposite of what they're feeling and having to recite too many scripted and phony responses.

When this happens, it's tragic, but all is not lost. The yellow pages can sometimes be all the resources one needs for help and a few phone calls to some great divorce attorneys can quickly help the Asperger regain herself and her sanity. Miscellaneous magazines at the store checkout stand with valuable articles like "How to Break Up with a Friend" might be good items to include with baby carrots on the grocery list. And it never hurts to imitate a certain fast food commercial to express yourself. "Oh, hi boss and co-workers I really don't care for and I no longer have to pretend to be friendly to because I've found a new opportunity. I'm just here to get my last cup of free coffee from the kitchen."

Brutal Honesty (aka Rudeness)

"Wow, they've got a nice place," says Jack as he and the wife drive by the luxury condo community with only enough space for a bachelor. "If anything ever happens to you and the kids, I'm moving there."

There's honesty. And then there's brutal honesty. Too often the Asperger exhibits too much of the latter.

Since Asperger people would rather be truthful, it never fails that sometimes that truth hurts. Or just pisses someone off. The Asperger is so focused on stating what is true, he or she cannot foresee how the truth might affect the other person's feelings. Like equating the loss of the wife and kids to an opportunity to live in a community with doorstop laundry service, fitness centers with rock climbing facilities and sparkling pools and saunas readily decked out with sexy, young ladies in bikinis that—unfortunately—one day will be responsible for moving you out of paradise and into a suburb with a minivan fit for four.

Yes, if you are ever interested in knowing if your butt really is too big, just ask an Asperger. And then you will learn never to ask again.

Brutal honesty, known to neurotypicals as rudeness, often crops its head in personal conversation, but it can manifest itself in various other situations.

Political discussions are never sparing, but the Asperger almost always appears as the radical, making his views known about not feeding the hungry so, "they will starve to death and we'll have fewer people to worry about feeding."

Brutal honesty can be direct, as the examples above, but also indirect, as in the form of an insulting compliment like, "Wow, you look so much prettier than the last time I saw you," or, "I'm really surprised your boobs are still full, considering most big ones like yours get flat at your age. I wonder when yours will start to go south," to, "Just wait until we have our children. You're going to have stretch marks to map the entire state. You may be lucky enough to avoid them with the first child, but by the second...no way."

Brutal honesty rears its head in both public and private conversation, small settings and large, at the most inappropriate times. "Should you really be wearing white considering everything I know you did in college?" the Asperger asks the bride during the reception in front of the groom, the bride and groom's parents and a dozen other guests.

In summary, Asperger people remind us that if you really don't want to know, don't ask.

Electronic Communication: Email, IM and Texting, Oh My

You know that guy. Like many Asperger people, he shies away from oral communication and speaks his mind with the keyboard. He thinks texting should be a recognized foreign language. He might text his wife when she's cooking in the kitchen at home when he's a long distance away—such as the bedroom upstairs. He will engage in a 20 minute back and forth email conversation when it could have been done face to face in five. Especially considering his office is right next door to yours. So close, you can even hear him typing his next response.

Asperger people are notoriously known for their preference to communicate through media other than saying it to your face. Sometimes the regular mode that neurotypicals use to communicate are problematic for the Asperger as there are always issues to keep in the back of one's mind besides the conversation—working harder to read facial expressions, respecting personal space, making enough eye contact to not let on that you're bored, etc.

To circumvent this problem, Asperger people use various electronic forms of communication to get the conversation going. And continuing.

Online dating was probably invented by an Asperger.

The romantic partner of an Asperger might find themselves frequently engaged in hot, passionate, amorous activity with the

Asperger wearing nothing but his wireless mouse. After protesting that he only talks to her on instant messenger when he wants to talk dirty for hours, he may defensively say he is performing his "manly duties" and couples should be romantic regularly. After ~~stalking~~ research reveals no other female in the picture, she may gently remind him of the fact that since they've been dating, they rarely have any face to face encounters. It's hard to stay romantic when you never see a person, you know.

Not to fear, as this is no barrier the relationship cannot overcome. That's why web cams were invented.

II.

Work—School and Environment

Internal Motivation

If you want to motivate a neurotypical to do something, you can offer numerous positive reinforcements such as money, recognition, your approval and respect. If you want to motivate an Asperger who doesn't want to do something, good luck. No, scratch that. No luck, just keep your money and your mouth to yourself and find someone else to do the job.

It's a well-known fact among those they live, work and play with, an Asperger is 99% internally motivated and 1% internally motivated to appear as if they are externally motivated.

The Asperger is motivated by his own set of morals, rules and standards for how things should be done. They are also motivated by what they feel will be a good outcome based on their efforts put forward.

Provided financial need is not an issue, an Asperger would rather spend twice as long working at a job they enjoy and find rewarding (like the special interest) than get paid more to work less in a much more boring job (like one that doesn't involve the special interest).

Kids pay attention in class, do their homework and get good grades for a variety of reasons. Some want to do the "right thing." Some want to avoid punishment from their parents. Some want to feel smart. Asperger kids may only want to do well in classes they find interesting and it may be extremely hard to convince them to make effort in subjects they don't like.

Being internally motivated may serve the Asperger well when being passionate about a particular subject is required for a goal, such as completing a degree in a certain field, specializing in a certain technical career or spending hours reading hundreds of papers on one single protein they're writing a thesis on.

This internal motivation is 99% a blessing and 1% a curse for Aspergers. It is 100% a curse for everyone else who wants them to do something they don't want to do.

Completing

The old saying is if you want something done, you ask a busy person.

The new saying is if you want something completed, you ask an Asperger person.

Aspergers dislike leaving work unfinished and often have an intense urge to complete a task, letting no distraction sway them from the course.

The insatiable urge to get the job done can take place during conversation, such as getting as much detail as possible into a 5-minute monologue about their area of interest. It may be in the form of completing a clerical or technical assignment, doing something creative or even reading something of interest.

Rain and snow doesn't keep the mailman away, and neither minor nor major distractions break the Asperger's train of thought. This includes people yawning and desperately trying to interrupt to add to the conversation. When the tornado strikes and whisks everyone away from their desks, the Asperger will add the last graph to the spreadsheet just before being dumped onto a tree branch, computer still on lap, file saved not a moment too late.

Somewhere in the brain, the intense spells to read a number of paragraphs or chapters, complete a certain number of problems, or seal a particular number of envelopes, must function to shut off any unnecessary functions that would cause the Asperger to leave the task before he/she feels it is time for a break. Hunger pangs persist. Blood sugar is dropping. Yet, the Asperger marches on with the PowerPoint slideshow.

Shifting back and forth in the chair to keep from wetting himself because he refuses to even walk three steps to his bedroom bathroom until he memorizes the last slide for the presentation, the Asperger blocks out dogs barking, children crying and his significant other ~~bitching, complaining~~, reminding him of his shared duties as a member of the household.

Printed Instructions

When giving an Asperger instruction or something new to learn, it's preferable that you give these instructions on paper. This way, they can always refer to this hard copy to remind you of the rules when you decide to change course or spend great time correcting all your spelling and grammar mistakes.

On a more serious note, Aspies find it much easier to complete a task or follow instructions either at work or school when the instructions are written vs. oral for several reasons.

One, even a neurotypical may find it difficult to get every detail of the order right when it's coming from the teacher or manager who gets by on four hours of sleep every night and thinks eight cups of coffee a day is a good substitute for using water to stay hydrated. Not only can people talk too fast, they also expect other people to understand exactly what they mean when they emphasize certain words, use certain inflections or particular tones. All while speaking at four times the average number of words spoken per minute, being revved up by the 7th of 8th cup of daily caffeine.

Many educators have become aware of this and are advising instructors to shy away from oral communication with the Asperger, especially when changing direction or instructions.

Smart instructors, having informed themselves of the best way to help an Asperger achieve her potential, will do this.

The alternative is engaging in a long, bitter discussion during office hours over an in-class announcement changing a paper's due date from the one clearly marked on the syllabus—the holy grail of printed instructions in the world of academia.

Perfectionism

Perfection is great when solving for a detailed math problem or getting the right measurements to design a building, so it won't fall over like a big Lego block. That's why perfectionism is great for some careers Aspergers choose like architect or engineering.

For the rest of the 99% of the vocations and life experiences an Asperger has, however, perfection doesn't really offer much help other than to give you an excuse to avoid some social event because you're at home revising the same paragraph for the 225th time for the week and not even close to being done.

An Asperger will often aim for no less than whatever is considered perfect for the task they need to accomplish. This can take the form of scoring a certain number of points, constructing the perfect object, designing the exact design needed or insisting that every page in a paper is written well the first time. Obviously, this is stressful and thinking of the punishment you might give yourself for being only 99% correct is enough to make you not even want to begin a task. Which leads to the other dirty "P" word—procrastination.

With mistakes comes learning, so it's not surprising that so many Aspies are well-adjusted people who manage to acquire many life experiences, skills and talents. If it were up to the Aspie, her own birth would be delayed by at least 30 years in order to make the perfect entry into the world. At some point in early childhood, they must have decided that the only way to move forward with anything was to forgive themselves for falling down a few times when learning to walk. But not that many times.

What is perhaps even more frustrating to an Asperger with perfectionist tendencies is the reaction they get from others who don't understand the reason behind it. Taking three hours to complete a task that normally takes one may mistakenly cause a co-worker or manager to believe the reports are out of the Asperger's range of work abilities. Silly people. They would never understand how important it is to choose the right font and narrowing things down from Arial to Arial Black to Arial Narrow to Arial Unicode MS is what draws the line between a great employee and an insanely neurotic one.

That line, however, is extremely thin. And would take hours to measure over and over again with multiple instruments before deciding upon the "right" value.

Imposing Morals in the Workplace

Being extremely moralistic people, Aspergers prefer to spend their days among those who agree with them and share their beliefs. Since many people spend their days earning a paycheck, albeit a lousily low one, the workplace is where an Asperger especially needs to feel he is surrounded by the most moral people who are practicing the best morals from the time they punch the clock in to leaving the parking lot.

As expected, this leads to problems.

An Asperger will often clash with someone at work with different morals than she or he. If he is in a superior position to that scumbag of an unholy, immoral person, he may use the almighty book of rules, otherwise known as management guidelines, to enforce his morals. This is done by making up new rules at work or prohibiting people from doing things at work that don't align with the Asperger's values.

There is good to having someone in power expect high standards from everyone beneath her. There has been great harm induced on others when people have just maintained status quo or done things as they're normally done without questioning. Those who challenge the status quo often incite change for the better. It's great to implement recycling and the use of biodegradable disposable silverware in the cafeteria if you're an environmentalist. It's good to remind everyone to turn off the smaller lights in their cubicles and power the computers to an energy saving setting before leaving. It's another thing for the recyclopath to hold week-ly meetings during which every team member must confess their sins of printing off emails, sharing exactly how many emails were printed during the week, how they contributed to the destruction of trees and making the biggest eco-sinner put their picture by the printer to remind everyone each item they print is being recorded and judgement day might come for them too the following week.

Teamwork—Avoiding It

To summarize how teamwork and the Asperger are related, consider this quote from *Dilbert* cartoonist Scott Adams:

"Water is good for you. Unless you're at the bottom of the ocean with an anchor tied to your ankle. Teamwork is like that. It can be a good thing, but more often it's like trying to breathe underwater."

One complaint some employers have about their Aspie employees is that they don't contribute to the team as much as desired. There are numerous reasons for this, and in many cases, it's not even the Asperger that's the problem.

There are instances when teamwork is a very positive experience for an Aspie. This is usually the case when the Aspie is working with people with comparable skills as her. This often isn't the case when an Asperger is forced to work on a team.

The best way for an Asperger to earn the title of being the greatest team player is to avoid hurting someone's feelings. This means never mentioning to them that they or their ideas are wrong or inefficient, especially if it means suggesting one of your brilliant ideas in place of one of their moronic ones.

Many times, the Asperger will be the member of the team who is the most excited about the project and will want to give 180%. This is a good thing, because most of the other team players will be giving about 25% of their effort, the other 75% being put into chit chat and small talk. The Asperger, thinking she is being a good team player, will casually remind everyone else about deadlines and staying on task. It's only later during a performance review by some of the wisest wizards known as management, does she learn this is displaying horrible teamwork skills and the best leader's job is to expect 10% from each person and preserve their self-esteem by letting them waste everyone else's 90% time.

Sometimes, the Asperger is the only one on the team to not understand what teamwork means. To them, it means dividing up a task among several different people so that each person does a different task and gets the whole job done as a team. In the world of business, teamwork often means everyone working on the same task (often being given the exact same list of tasks by the boss). This ensures that if anyone does a poor or incomplete job, at least one other person who has the same task as they do does the half they didn't do. When the fractions don't add up and nothing gets done, don't remind anyone of this because it means you offend them or hurt their feelings—which is the best way to hurt your performance review.

It's never a good idea to stay totally quiet during group meetings and activities because you'll be accused of not contributing. It's never a good idea to contribute to group meetings and activities because you'll be accused of talking too much about your ideas and being abrasive and trampling over others, even if they happen to be the ideas that will make the project work.

It's always good to protect everyone's feelings.

Keep doing these things and you're sure to earn the title of most valuable employee with no value by the end of the month.

Closed Doors

Aspergers love keeping the door to their bedroom or office closed. And they love slamming the door in your face when you're trying to enter the "zone" to discuss anything non-important (i.e. things they don't want to talk about) almost as equally.

While neurotypicals see a closed door as cutting off communication or making them feel unwelcome, the Asperger will describe a room shut off from the outside world as a solace, a way to avoid sensory disturbances like the sounds of someone's bad '80s music radio station at their cubicle, workplace gossip or family members wanting to interrupt to discuss all things touchy-feely and interpersonal doing work or leisure activities.

Occasionally, there are a few people that the closed-door policy does not apply to. They're usually four-legged people.

Those who know the Asperger's closed-door policy but do not understand the need for a private, enclosed space to function often wonder or gossip what he or she could possibly be doing that is so secretive. Is she really working or using company time to shop online? I heard he takes off his clothes in there. The au naturel rumor is one rumor an Asperger will want to confirm, as it ensures he'll never be disturbed by one of his co-workers taking the liberty to open the door without asking.

Becoming a Professor

Many Asperger people choose to pursue careers in academia. Often, the academic area of interest is a special interest or something that was a special interest growing up. For this reason, becoming a professor is much like a "Revenge of the Asperger Nerds" experience.

In the old pre-PhD days, the Asperger had to find someone willing to put up with her endless hours of "drosophila fly mating" facts. When the Asperger became a professor, she found joy in knowing not only was she able to discuss the sexual behavior of flies and get paid for it, people were willing to pay thousands of dollars and go into debt to hear her speak about it and obtain a piece of paper stating they too were credentialed in fly sex.

Great pleasure is taken in giving 2-hour speeches where students are now at the Asperger's mercy—forced to take notes, maybe even pretend they are interested and ask questions if participation points are included in the grading system. The Asperger professor loves giving telephone book sized notes and telling her students, "No cherry picking will take place," as any ridiculous fly sex fact she loves to bring up at all the good parties may also be placed on a test.

The Asperger professor will eventually become tenured after publishing dozens of papers about her voyeuristic fly sex experiences and being given lots of money by groups like the National Institutes of Health and various other organizations she has convinced through careful con-artist intellectualizing (otherwise known as grant writing) studying fly sex will save the world. Or the children. Or the whales. It really just depends on the organization and how much money they're willing to give her.

Finally, the tenured professor job is the opportunity for the Asperger to prove (at least to herself) why she was put on the earth and that descriptions used to label her years ago (pedantic, little professor syndrome) by professionals that were obviously not as bright as her seem perfectly befitting and not insulting or abnormal at all. "Pedantic is good," she thinks. "People are inherently stupid, and it is my job to teach them. Or at least force them to experience many sleepless nights memorizing fly sex facts."

Becoming an Engineer,
Being an Enginerd

Right up there with becoming a professor, the career choice for many Aspergers is engineering. People who are engineers are more likely to have a child or a grandchild on the autistic spectrum so there may be something in the genes. If you're operating a piece of electrical equipment or driving down the freeway, you probably have an Asperger to thank or not thank, depending on if the freeway was designed with the town's flooding tendencies in mind.

Engineers are usually not your party people. Engineering is a most nerdy profession and many Aspergers enjoy this, because at least it flatters their intellect to know they are in a very mentally challenging profession. Some have been nicknamed "enginerds." Career planning may take place when the Asperger asks him or herself: What kind of enginerd should I be? Depending on the precise algorithm of nerdiness and weirdness, there are several categories to choose from. Here are a few examples of the possibilities:

Biomedical/Biochemical: Not as nerdy as some other areas. Incorporating medicine into their interest may win points with nerdy, but cooler pre-med students. People are always interested in others who can make food taste better, last longer and stick extra preservatives in them that they cannot pronounce. Ability to bring about advancements in pharmaceuticals may also impress hot nurses.

Civil: Middle of the road nerds. Not quite as cool as the bio-medical/biochemical enginerds. Usually possess good enough social skills to trick some neurotypicals to marry them, the neurotypicals thinking this is the way math and science geeks behave. And size does matter. If you can design a really tall, big, fancy building you will be elevated to stardom status among enginerds and regular people.

Electrical: Level extreme nerdiness. Just plain weird. Even Steve Urkel crosses the street to avoid them.

III.

Relationships

Wives as Secretaries

Some Aspergers may have problems with what is known as executive functioning. Executive functioning consists of skills like planning.

As children, Aspergers have their mothers or fathers to step in and remind them when their executive functions aren't functioning like they should—reminding them to do homework, mapping out their schedules, color coding important items, etc. Essentially, they take the role of a secretary.

Except for those who still live with mom at 45 (Which is completely okay. Who wouldn't want free meals?), as the Asperger grows older, the secretary mom is retired, and secretary wife takes her place.

A woman who dates an Asperger man may want to learn the signs of men who like secretaries, not just because it will help her understand why mom still sends notes with stickers in her son's lunch every day when he goes to his job as a head software developer, but because she may one day become that secretary should she choose to marry that Asperger man.

Living with mom is a #1 sign, as it enables the Aspie man to be within a few feet of his much-needed assistant. Mom will most likely be involved with his daily personal activities (laundry, meals), but might take on extended duties to organize his social activities as well. Don't be surprised if the secretary takes on expanded duties and serves as a screener for his personal life, interviewing you, asking tough questions and taking notes that she will later use to

~~demand~~ make suggestions as to how appropriate you are as a future secretary. Be sure to welcome her advice and her presence as often as possible in order to get the best learning experience that will enable you to raise all the future children in your family—including the child that magically is around the same age as you that you exchanged vows with. Invite the secretary to all events you and your significant other partake in. Except the bedroom. Okay, invite her to the bedroom—you'll need someone to make the bed and tidy up. But kick her out for any other activities because that would be TOO freaky. A romantic "don't forget to" list written by mom is more organization than even an Asperger is looking for.

Admin wife will provide services for the Asperger like wardrobe matching for the stylistically challenged and reminding him not to dump the cup of punch back into the bowl after he's drank from it during the corporate company party.

Sometime after marriage, feeling as if they've given birth to a 180-pound child, the wife may become frustrated playing the role of mother, especially if she's already playing mother to several underaged children who need secretaries.

In most cases, when mothers are looking for help outside the home, they hire a nanny. If looking after an adult is similar to parenting another child, why should this situation be any different?

Like many situations where women hire other women to come into their homes and work with their husbands, the wife should be careful in who will be her outside help. Only certain individuals will be highly qualified. The wife could consider hiring another secretary, but she should only hire one that is extremely ugly, filled with warts, 80-years old or not interested in the opposite sex. It may be easier to hire a gay man. If the outside help offends him by not liking or putting down his special interest, there will be ZERO chances of any blossoming extramarital affair.

Late Marriages and Partnerships

Ladies, the 40-year old still living with his mother may be a man to steer clear of, but he may also be your Asperger knight in shining armor with a collection of fake medieval swords so large, he's turned his mother's garage into a museum.

Many Aspergers marry much later than neurotypicals. Again, this is another example of how culture shapes how normal the Aspie is or isn't. An Asperger man living in the United States may suffer ridicule for his mom still doing his laundry. But in Italy, men commonly live with their mammas throughout their 30s and 40s, the mother still making dominant decisions in their lives.

Part of the reason Aspergers marry later in life is due to maturity. While a 25-year old NT male lets the woman of his interest know he's got a thing for her by inviting her to dinner, a 25-year old Asperger throws spitballs across his cubicle to annoy her.

Aspergers who are competitive in their careers will also delay marriage, as it's more important to finish the PhD or sell the million-dollar business before settling down with a wife who can't understand why 16 hours a day must be spent on work.

Aspies are also very specific about their mate choices. Unless you've signed up for a dating site for drag queens, it may be hard to find a "redhead, master's degree, who's over six feet tall." Still, the Aspie isn't one to settle and will wait until he's caught his "nurse in pediatrics," "someone educated in social sciences who likes animals" or "someone who will organize my life like a secretary" is found.

NT friends and family often have excessive interest in setting up the Aspie with potential date mates. This may be due to their worries about the Aspie being single and alone or their inability to see the Aspie isn't interested in dating. At least not interested in dating the drunks the NT friends attempt to set them up with. And despite their confidence in "helping" the Aspie, many of these NTs are in no way suitable to find matches for their Aspie friends. Since the Aspie prides herself on deciding who the appropriate authority figures are, she may have already decided that women who rival Elizabeth Taylor in marriages before 35 are not the best relationship experts. In addition, the Aspie does not have the same needs of constant companionship the NT has and doesn't mind living in solitude. In other words, they are not the needy girlfriends who flock to the bar like a magnet every weekend in hopes of finding a mate. Note: This is where the NT girlfriend finds the flood of drunks to set the Asperger up with. If, after a week, things don't work out...say hello to my single friend.

One must understand they will always be behind others in relationship development. By the time they've finally "tied the knot," most neurotypicals will already be ahead of the game—and on their 2nd divorce.

Weird Concepts of Love

Often when an Asperger is in a relationship with a neurotypical, the NT partner may complain that the Asperger doesn't readily show love and affection.

It would help tremendously if the Asperger could at least define love in a language spoken by most on the planet, which rarely happens.

This may be because being an Asperger makes one naturally different in how love and feelings are expressed or because the Aspie has a hard time describing something so abstract.

When a neurotypical gives a definition of love, it's usually something that sounds like text from a Hallmark card, flowing smoothly and initiating feelings of warmth among even the grumpiest of Scrooges.

"Love is caring for my partner during hard and easy times and reassuring him/her how valuable he/she is to me," one neurotypical may remark. Or the NT may use adjectives to describe love such as "patient," "non-judgmental," "affectionate" or "passionate."

The Asperger's definition is a completely different story:

The Practical: "Love is doing the dishes daily, so my spouse doesn't yell."

The Dreamer: "Love is what I will experience one day. Soon, I hope."

The Honest One: "I don't know."

The Brutally Honest One: "I don't care."

The Asperger doesn't have or recognize the need to continually tell the partner he or she is important and may believe once "I love you" is said once, there's no need to keep saying it again. Or they may believe love is demonstrated by doing something nice for the person regularly.

To top off the obvious oral communication issues, let's not forget the Asperger may not enjoy giving or receiving traditional gestures of love such as touching or hugging. And Aspergers may not realize that traditional gestures of love and affection shown by an NT are meant to convey such meaning.

"When I work late, she waits until I'm home to have dinner? Maybe she's just hungry later on those days too."

[Insert the Homer Simpson "D'oh" here or any other time the Asperger just doesn't seem to get it.]

The Asperger language of love may still need some deciphering but one thing's for sure. Given the fact Aspies value their alone time so much, if an Aspie chooses to include you in her/his time, she/he must have some feeling for you.

Otherwise, you and your possessions would be kicked to the curb to make room for the collection of international telephone books.

Not Valuing Traditional Standards in Romantic Partners

Yet another area where Aspergers seem to contradict themselves is the area of dating/finding a mate. Although they can be very particular about the type of partner they want and may set high standards for finding someone, many of them also tend to care less about the standards many neurotypicals set. They connect with intellect and shared interests as much as they do physically.

It's a known fact that Aspergers may be less likely to care about particular physical features. They are also less likely to demand a partner with the same background, culture and age and date someone several years younger or older.

You heard right cougars. Ready, set, pounce.

If you're a 50-year old woman who's eyeing a much younger Aspie man, Demi Moore may have nothing on you.

Because they are often immature and may lack the strong ability to do many organizational things with their lives, they may also search for a motherly figure to move in with. Another advantage to pursuing the older woman since she will already have some spare rooms in her home now that the children are off to college.

Who knows why an Asperger is less concerned with so many of the requirements NTs set in stone when finding a mate? Perhaps it's because so many of these factors are heavily defined by social norms, something the Asperger has no intuitive understanding of. They wonder why lots of money is so important, especially if the person is bright, educated enough to learn new trades and has steady employment with benefits. They feel there are many nice boys out there vs. just the "nice Jewish boys" grandmother insists they must find. They can't understand other men's obsession with large breasts. Okay, so as males, Asperger or neurotypical, they at least understand that.

Instead of needing to find a single white Protestant, aged 25-45, fit build, never married, liberal from the east coast, the Asperger is simply looking for a caring, loyal, analytical person with strong values who will tolerate their intense need to collect stamps.

Could a romantically unhappy neurotypical take a cheap lesson from an Asperger instead of throwing all their money on therapy, dating clubs and hair plugs?

Embarrassing Children

All parents will embarrass their children at one point or another. Asperger parents will embarrass their children at many more points along the line, especially if the children are neurotypical.

This often happens when the parent is interacting with the child's friends and acting even weirder than most parents do. They may try to impress the other children with their effortful, but horrible grasp on slang, which may even result in a phone call from the other parent questioning why an adult would say something so inappropriate to a minor. The slang was completely cool in the '50s but means something completely different now.

The child of an Aspie may suddenly want to crawl under a rock when his father greets his friends because Aspie Dad isn't good at moderating his small talk for different age groups. So, he shakes the 8-year old's hand and asks him, "What do you do with your days?"

Um...video games. Ride the bicycle. Etch-a-sketch. Sometimes all three during an intense day away from the classroom.

It could be dressing even more weirder than regular parents.

It could be forgetting to put on clothes while they're lounging in the backyard enclosed by a tall fence because they've forgotten Thursdays are the days classmates come over and the first thing they do is head for the back door where the pool is.

Aspie parents should not lose any more sleep than a neurotypical does from worrying about everything scarring children for life. Will the children grow up happy? Yes. Will they have a good sense of self-respect, self-esteem and be goal oriented? Yes. Will they be accepted by their peers and have a circle of those peers they hold near and dear, spend quality time with and consider best friends? Of course! Just don't expect those friends to come over to use the backyard pool too often.

Marriages to People
from Other Countries

Aspergers often form romantic relationships and marry people from foreign countries or cultures different from their own. This may be due to several reasons. Countries other than the Asperger's native one may not have the same social rules that normally hinder his interaction with people and cause social awkwardness. People from countries outside of his own will often attribute an Asperger's social differences to cultural or simply not care. It's important that the Asperger recognize this trait early on and realize the advantages and potential problems it could bring.

Dating and marrying a foreign person can be an exhilarating and satisfying experience, but like any relationship, it must be taken with caution. Aspergers can be naïve in relationships and may not recognize a potential predatory partner with interests other than love and companionship. Cultural differences between partners may present an exciting learning experience for both, but eventually some differences that are very culturally based (worship practices, gender roles, raising children) may present problems in long-term relationships.

But once an Asperger male or female masters love street smarts, he or she learns the advantages of intercultural love far outweigh the risks of things going sour and should jump right on it, wasting no time in finding a partner from overseas or across the border. No stone should be left unturned, no opportunity missed. Take as many foreign language classes as possible in high school, college and from the University of French in Five Weeks from Books on Audiotape. Join culture clubs, both for learning about the world around you and checking out the European hottie down the street from you.

While still living at home with the parents, encourage them to host a foreign exchange student, preferably multiple and all of the particular gender you are interested in. You might even try to convince your guests it is custom for the exchange student to marry the son/daughter of the host 5-10 years down the line, much like arranged marriages in other countries. Say it was written in the exchange contract and approved by the school. Heck, say it's the law—do you really think 16-year-olds have bothered memorizing every one before they came over here?

Different Couple Living Arrangements

Contrary to what some think, Aspergers do indeed get married and have families. However, these living arrangements may be a little different than your neurotypical situation. Due to the Asperger's intense need for solitude and being left alone for a good portion of the day, Asperger people may not interact with their neurotypical or even fellow Asperger partner in a manner that is normally expected.

For example, an Asperger may say to his/her partner, "I like to have a lot of alone time. So, just because we're in the house together, doesn't mean we have to interact." There may be arrangements of sleeping in separate beds, eating alone versus together and in some cases, even having two completely separate homes or apartments even though they are married.

Although the neurotypical spouse may not even know why the Asperger partner is so damn weird, he/she may very well adapt and try to understand, thus having an unwritten agreement between the two. However, it never fails that some nosy neurotypicals with no lives will find out about the "weirdness at 2525 Otherwise Non-Freaky Neighborhood Lane" and begin to talk. They may start to have "heart-to-heart," which is more like "head-butt to head-butt" conversations with the neurotypical and Asperger partner, desperately trying to incite change even when both partners are happy.

Truth be told, these neurotypicals are just jealous. Susie wouldn't mind peace and quiet versus a groping and demanding husband at home every evening at 7:00 p.m. Harry down the street knows he too could benefit from a separate bed and thus avoiding his wife's jittery restless legs kicking him in the crotch every morning or being awoken by her loud farts in the middle of the night. But remember, neurotypicals care too much about what is socially proper. Either that or Harry is looking for a way out of the 4th child he promised his wife.

Dating Themselves

Someone once said, "Love thyself." This motto is good for anyone to live by, but Asperger people take the advice one step further: love thyself and date thyself.

How would you describe a person who dates himself? Narcissistic? Strange? Nonsense! It's simply relationship heaven for Asperger people. Since they enjoy solitude so much, it's no surprise Aspergers often choose to go solo during many social activities. Unlike neurotypicals, they freely partake in movie outings, dinners, museum visits, concerts—you name it—without worrying about having someone to accompany them. Asperger people love to date themselves! Aspergers find nothing odd about this practice and are quite surprised to learn neurotypicals have completely different viewpoints.

In conversation, an Asperger person might ask [insert neurotypical X] if she went to see the musical *Jersey Boys.* A neurotypical person might reply with, "No, I was going to go, but I couldn't find anyone to go with me."

"How ridiculous," the Asperger person thinks to herself. "Why would anyone miss out on so much fun just because they can't find anyone to go with them?"

The older the Asperger person gets, the more she learns just how ridiculous this neurotypical rule applies to "the others," from shopping to sports games to relieving oneself in the lavatory. As a result, the Asperger vows to live life even fuller, trying her hardest never to miss any fun because everyone else's calendar is full, no one else likes similar types of movies or no one else at the dinner table has the urge to tinkle.

And dating oneself has tons of perks for the Asperger as he never has to compromise on when, where and what to do. This ensures that most dates can involve the special interest and the date can never complain about going to the same restaurant every Friday night, using this as an example to bring up "inflexibility" in couples' therapy or bash him in front of their girlfriends about the lack of "spontaneity" in the relationship.

Naturally, safety should always be considered when dating oneself and dates in places like dark streets or deserted areas aren't desirable. The Asperger female unfortunately will find herself surrounded by various male "friends" if she chooses to take herself on a date to a bar where the social rule followed by drunken neurotypical males is to offer her a drink in hopes she will break up with herself and date them. Yes, cautions of dating oneself should not be taken lightly. Always meet yourself in a public place. Email is good but give yourself your phone number only if you feel comfortable.

Much neurotypical chatter will always take place about Aspergers known to date themselves. If you could Google this chatter, keywords might be "isolated" or "loner" or "I never see her with anyone." But the next time a nosy neurotypical poses one of the most annoying questions, "Are you even dating anyone?" quickly turn to her and say, "Darn right. I'm dating myself."

IV.

Thoughts and Their Processes

Assuming Everyone's a Mind Reader

Because of theory of mind issues (not being able to easily predict and interpret what another person's thoughts or motives are), Aspergers may take on what appears to be an "assume you are a mind reader" approach in social interactions.

On some disastrous occasions, the Asperger will assume someone important to him already knows things gone unsaid (such as expressions of love).

He/she may not show up to a date and not bother to call before or after.

When questioned about his disappearance, he may innocently say something like, "I assumed you figured something came up."

As expected, this goes over quite well...right.

Of all the things his date could assume, an unexpected event is the last.

Assumed he dumped her for an evening with the guys. Yes.

Assumed he traded her night for a night with some other woman from the office. Yes.

Assumed he doesn't value her time and doesn't have to call in advance to change plans. Yes.

If he's really, really good at assumptions though, he should definitely assume she'll be making nasty comments about being stood up on her Facebook status.

Not Getting the Big Picture

If the devil is in the details, the Asperger has found a way to camouflage its horns much like some have successfully camouflaged their Asperger's syndrome. An Asperger consciousness is a huge sponge that absorbs everything—whether they want to or not. And whether it's useful or not.

Some professionals call this having a "weak central coherence" or the inability to get the main idea from something and exclude unimportant details—see the "big picture."

In other words, it's why it takes Aspergers three weeks to complete a project their NT peers do in one day.

Researching and writing a one-page paper on whether the residents of a certain state usually vote Democrat or Republican is easy if you find a stat on the percentage of blue/red voters in the state. It's not so easy when you discover a book of original research journals at the library which review political party preference by various factors like age and gender, which leads you to research how each demographic in the state has voted in the past 50 years, which leads you to your desire to include these stats in the paper that has already reached three pages, which—in a sleepless night of curiosity—leads you to accidentally discover a paper on unexpected election outcomes in the region of the country you're writing about. After all, it wouldn't paint a fair picture of party preference in the state if you didn't write at least five paragraphs on the anomalies that have occurred. Then there's a paper that discusses party preference for people who rarely vote. So, the stats you have for party preference of voters isn't inclusive enough and you need to balance those with people in the same state that always vote. And break these results up by each socioeconomic category possible, because lumping everyone into blue vs. red doesn't take into account how rich women with naturally colored red hair who dye it blue and hold at least a master's degree always vote against the way the state in which they reside does.

Oh, no. How will you condense your 25-page paper into one that was supposed to discuss—GENERALLY—voter preferences for people in Massachusetts?

J.F. Browne

Details

Take a neurotypical outside and ask her to describe what she sees. She'll probably give you a basic summary like a brick house with a couple of trees in the front yard and a blue car parked in the driveway. Put an Aspie in front of the same setting and she'll tell you how many stories the house has, whether it looks like real brick or façade, the type of trees planted in the yard, whether or not leaves are on them, the make and model of the car, any species of plants growing in the garden, the squirrel in the tree and which tree the squirrel sits in (relative to some other landmark, like the one closest to the parked car) and the cat who sits on the steps so still it almost looks like a statue but licks itself from time to time to let you know it isn't.

Aspies have a great ability to see things others don't see, remember obscure facts that may or may not be important to the scenario and in general, give the little things much more attention than neurotypicals do.

It's interesting, because although there is plenty of data showing many Aspies are females, Aspergerness is still thought of as a male-dominated syndrome. But isn't it funny how in the neurotypical world, it's usually the females who remember all the details? Especially the ones the males, neurotypical or not, don't want them to retain. Like how you screwed up 20 years ago and forgot her birthday, making it the absolute worst day of her life. Or when you screwed up the anniversary 10 years ago, making it the second absolute worst day of her life.

But there are more details to recall than those good for bringing up during every couple fight. Fascinating rules, patterns, sequences and numbers are as much of a turn-on for the Aspie as the lingerie he bought for his wife that was several sizes too small—marking the third absolute worst day in her life that she will remember and remind him of for the rest of his life.

Concrete Versus Abstract Thinking

Right along the thinking continuum with taking things literally is the ability to think in abstract versus concrete. Aspies often have trouble with abstract thinking, which may make some of them more comfortable with academic subjects and careers that require exact or either/or answers. Math is great, but the literature class that asks them to constantly compare and contrast events or extract main and sub-ideas from the book or story are a real bummer.

An extremely concrete Aspie may spend hours on the phone with the IRS arguing over the concept of claiming dependents because she cannot imagine how the task of "claiming a dependent" can be restricted to a certain number of people. Either that or she is playing dumb to get more money.

"That doesn't make any sense," she might say. "Why can't I claim myself if my father claimed me as a dependent?"

"The rule is you cannot claim yourself if someone else can claim you as a dependent. But if I can be claimed by him, I should be able to be claimed by other people. So, I should be able to claim myself."

The problem with this abstract concept is that the Aspie cannot view "claiming a dependent" in terms of the task being something only one person can do. To her, claiming should be like humans smiling. If one human can smile, surely most humans can smile. So why would you restrict smiling (or the amount of refund money you get to spend in the spring) to one human?

Some Aspies have found ways to circumvent this problem by turning abstract ideas into concrete examples they can understand.

After going back and forth several times about this, it's certain that only one person would be able to smile during the conversation, and it's definitely not the agitated IRS operator unless little "dependent" statuettes can be given to the Aspie, taking them away once they are "claimed" to help her understand the concept.

Philosophizing

Little professor or little philosopher? Maybe a little bit of both.

It's been proposed that Aspergers are like little philosophizers in the manner in which they learn about the social world. Aspies spend so much time observing, taking notes and reflecting on their own and others' behaviors and motivations. After doing this so much, the inner thoughts of an Asperger may start to sound like something you'd read from a Philosophy 101 course.

Philosophizing has a definite link to Asperger females. Many Aspie boys demonstrate the stereotypical Asperger trait of reciting facts. Aspie females, on the other hand, will often replace this fact-citing trait with deep commentary about issues in life, drawing conclusions and pointing out links while explaining everything from human behavior to business.

Just like philosophers sat around in their favorite same robes and discussed what it meant to be human, to think and to love, the Asperger may be caught wearing their favorite pair of pants regularly and making conclusions about how people associate, rules for friendships, romantic relationships and work relations.

The philosophizing Aspie will examine the culture at her workplace and in a moment of deep thought, proclaim, "Men and women differ in their expectations and what constitutes poor performance in the office. With men, it is the presence of a behavior (being late) that results in reprimand. With women, it's often the absence of a behavior (alienating co-workers) that brings the re-buke of management. "

Or, in more modern philosophical terms, "Stupid bitches that get me in trouble in the office are so needy, you can't get any peace or work done because they constantly need to tell you about their weekend."

I think...therefore I am Aspie.

Mental Olympics

Because so many Aspergers have clumsiness issues and can barely execute complicated eye-hand coordination movements, it's safe to say most won't be contenders at the Olympics. But that doesn't mean they can't score a gold medal in another set of games where the ability to recall the events of the day, worry about them, worry about the possible things that could go wrong with these events and then worry how to handle it, can persuade even the toughest judge to bump a 9.9 to a 10. Because of a less than athletic theory of mind, much of an Asperger's energy is often spent figuring out the meaning behind others' actions or words and worrying. At the end of the day, the Asperger has used his mind—although quite large and capable—so much he suffers from mental exhaustion. All Aspies do it to some degree. The ones that do it best could serve on Team Aspie in the Mental Olympics.

Life's day to day events create different categories of competition in the Mental Olympics. There's the Mental Meter Relay—how far you can carry a thought that continues to bog down your mind and make you tired. If you spend nine hours a day wondering how you will handle your in-laws during the holidays while your competitor spends a mere six, you will be crowned champion. There's also Mental Weight Lifting—how many different worries can you carry in your brain during a given day. The more problems and issues, the better competitor you are and more likely to take home a medal at the end of the day. Or fall asleep on the couch before you even finish reading the mail.

Like in other professional sports, the Asperger Mental Olympian will find his glory days coming to an end as he ages. The thoughts that once kept him up all night long he can only sustain for an hour or less a day because he has learned how to solve many of life's issues through lots of exposure to different problems and practice solving them. But that doesn't mean he won't occasionally bask in his prior accomplishments. He may think to himself: *In my younger years, there was a time when I could focus for three days in a row solely on figuring out what my wife meant to say during breakfast. As a retired champion, I know she meant nothing because she never makes sense, and now I am moving on to quickly solve the problem of how to pay for her hobby of shopping at antique malls.*

Worrying: Working the Wigdala

Have you worked your wigdala today? Sounds strange. Maybe even a little dirty. Let's explain with a brief lesson in Neuroscience 101.

The brain is divided into several areas, some of which are more responsible for some activities than others. The cerebellum, for example, is the hub for any athlete's success on the field, track and court. It controls complex motor functions of the skeletal muscular system, regulating your posture, balance and coordination during those movements. This fact alone leads some Aspergers to wonder what happened to theirs as their clumsiness can only leave them to hope for a Forrest Gump-like athleticism. Another function-controlling area of the brain would be the amygdala, which plays a role in regulating emotions. Then there is a similarly named center of the brain that has become a hot topic in research and will soon generate millions of dollars that intellectual con-artists—known as PhD grant writers—will snatch. That area, responsible for the center of worrying in Aspergers, is called the wigdala.

Aspergers worry a lot. Day in and day out. It's possible Aspergers worry in their sleep as well, but it's hard to document because a person's bedroom activities are a private matter. Usually. The Asperger will worry about every anticipated problem or situation that might come up and wonder how on earth they will deal with it. When a solution is not reached, they may worry that it's taking too long to come up with one. They worry that things might happen, things might not happen and how to make things happen.

All of these worries and fears result in a super wigdala or a wigdala on steroids. It has been increased significantly in size from being worked so hard, the Asperger finds himself wigged out (others use the terms physically and emotionally exhausted).

What some Aspergers need are slight boosts of confidence to remember the many times they have successfully dealt with any difficult situation that caused anxiety in the past. That's right. You own your wigdala; your wigdala does not own you! (Note: This is the point where usually you are asked to send $99.95 for a Wigdala Working Kit, complete with a pamphlet containing testimonials by people who've found success with the Wigdala Working Kit, but whose results are not typical.)

Positive wigdala working consists of simply remembering the times when the Asperger showed the wigdala who's boss. It might help to make a list of those events. And that's where Microsoft Excel comes in handy. With 65,536 rows and 256 columns, there are a total of 16,777,216 cells in one worksheet (which by the way is a great fact to recite to your fellow Asperger nerd friends with whom you often engage in speaking Factanese)! That's enough cells to document a whopping 3% of an Asperger person's daily worries and how she successfully—through hair pulling and nail biting—at the end of the day, made it through them.

Taking Things Literally

Once upon a time there was a young college Asperger student working as an assistant to a professor who was a very busy and prolific researcher. The student liked the job—good pay, close to home and school and was in the area of interest the student wanted to go into after graduation. But the biggest bonus of all was that the duties involved following lots of "to do" lists, which tickled the student pink. Much pleasure was derived from completing the lists, crossing items off the list and making sub-lists of things on previous lists that weren't complete and needed to be added to the current one.

One day the student was going through the list and found a personal favor the professor was requesting. In addition to photocopying handouts and doing literature searches, the student was instructed to find a "female doctor." Since there were no specifics, the student figured the professor needed all the options possible and spent the entire afternoon thumbing through the yellow pages, writing down the names of every female M.D. or D.O. with a name from Alice to Alejandra. After turning in the list, the student was shocked and a little embarrassed to discover the assignment had been completed incorrectly. The professor didn't care if her doctor was named Janet or John. She just needed a doctor for... the female region.

Like the student, Aspergers take things very literally. Don't bother communicating with them using hints, nuances, implications, euphemisms or slang because they probably won't get it and become quite frustrated. This in turn can cause problems for everyone involved, including you.

When you tell the Asperger person you'll call them back at 8:00 p.m., you better be sure your clocks are in synchronicity with theirs. A callback that occurs later than 8:00:09 p.m. warrants serious explaining and, "my clock is a minute or two slow," won't cut it.

An even better way to screw yourself over with the literal Asperger is to suggest something negative about them for not getting the hidden meaning by mentioning that it's, "common sense," or "not literally, of course," or even making threats you really don't plan on following through with. The word "lawsuit" dropped casually over the phone may send 3xs as many lawsuits your way once the Asperger person finds loopholes in your threat and takes action on it—even if you never intended to file anything and are just trying to figure a way to make him change his pain in the butt ways.

The Asperger may see these confusing and ego bruised moments as opportunities to put you at the end of their short-tempered correction stick: "She *is* a PhD. Why isn't she using the term "gynecologist?" You will be reminded of what is proper and what is not proper, how you are stupid for not being proper and they will call upon the proper authority resource to convince themselves everything is okay. The Asperger will then use those resources to reassure himself there was absolutely nothing stupid or silly about his interpretation. "The job description read "research assistant" not "personal assistant." Shouldn't be bringing up medical conditions in a workplace setting anyway. Violates the "welcoming co-worker environment" policy. Plus, I so, so didn't need to know about that."

V.

Hobbies/Special Interests/Leisure Activities

Interests in Other Cultures

Aspergers can naturally be called friends, lovers without borders.

They have a natural interest in other cultures and other countries. Such Asperger teenagers may be the ones to persuade their parents into hosting foreign exchange students. While the parent is concerned that the exchange student is of the same sex, the Asperger is looking for the exact opposite. This will guarantee a date to dances, proms and other school activities.

Some Aspergers will readily admit they prefer to date, befriend people from other countries. Such as people claim to be into blondes, curly haired women or even the "chubby chasers," an Asperger will readily admit during his teenage years he was, "chasing after the foreign exchange students." Students that were running...running very fast back to the airport once they learned of his fantasies of hosting a real Swiss Miss from Switzerland, complete with a sexy short skirt, low hanging blouse and hot chocolate spiked with something that's only legal for a minor to drink in the European country the student hails from.

Other cultures' social norms may be why Aspies get along well with people on opposite sides of the border. Not only do these cultures attribute the Aspie's strangeness as a "cultural difference," their idea of an ideal man or woman isn't nearly as superficial as it is in his own. A country where education and literacy are valued highly may be impressed at the Asperger's knowledge of obscure facts while those in his own country would roll their eyes.

As she grows older, the Aspie can further immerse herself in other cultures by studying foreign languages in school, pursuing a career in international affairs or one that requires extensive traveling abroad.

Ultimately, it may be a foreign person the Aspie chooses as the lifelong mate. And the lifelong person to provide the spiked hot chocolate in the morning.

Fantasy

Growing up, many people had a superhero they enjoyed imitating, in the form of playtime, learning about and dressing up as. Aspergers have superheroes and fantasies just like everyone else. Some may have fantasized about Xena Warrior Princess. And no, this isn't some man's fantasy that is created while entering data at his computer that he is being dominated by Lucy Lawless in a bustier.

Aspergers who enjoy fantasy worlds will often retreat to various forms of it such as science fiction, mythological characters and video games. They can take on the personas of characters, recite scripted fantasy conversations and relieve themselves from the stress of the real world.

Little Aspergers grow up to be big adults and may still retain fantasy interests, though thankfully tailoring them (usually) to a more appropriate level based on time, maturity and social constraints. The Superman costume is great for Halloween. It's even great for adult parties. Not so great for picking up sugar and flour. And no, wife doesn't really want to sleep with Superman.

Adults of today, both Asperger and neurotypical, can continue the fantasies they were forced to give up for reality. As long as no one else is standing behind the computer and they can ensure the IT department isn't snooping for management.

Music

An iPod used in moderation for entertainment is one thing. An iPod for life support is another.

For some Aspergers, music can serve as a special interest. Music can be used as a form of relaxation by listening, a hobby by playing or satisfying academic curiosity, such as studying music history.

In some Aspergers, it's quite easy to spot how much time this special interest dominates their lives. They are the ones who signed up for multiple music history courses in college, ranging from jazz to rock in the '70s. They also have every music website that allows for viewing videos or listening to songs bookmarked on their browsers. These online sources serve as traps for a music-loving Asperger, as they often make suggestions based on the current artist playing. Thus, "If you like ___, you'll like ___," results in clicking from link to link until an entire day is spent discovering new artists and not discovering the laundry. Their album collection rivals the stock of a national library, often reaching 100s or 1000s and needing separate storage just to accommodate the volume.

Elevator music, songs heard over loudspeakers in retail stores and on commercials lead to the discovery of new artists, which leads to more CDs and an ever expansion of their music education. Some may even sort the collection by time periods of their lives, like the teenage years vs. early twenties vs. mid-twenties.

One movie character whose music collection mirrored that of an obsessive music loving Aspie was the cranky, OCD writer Melvin Udall, played by Jack Nicholson in *As Good as It Gets*. Not only did he have his CDs organized in a particular manner, he had home-made mixes with labels indicating what purpose the CD served. Songs to "Get Things Done" and "Pep Things Up," were included with other collections that met lists of strict criteria of "use if" and "use when." Ironically, like an Aspie, this character has some routines he must strictly live by, such as eating breakfast at the same table at the same restaurant every day.

Solo Sports

Solitary sports offer an environment free of things that may distract or bother an Aspie, like loud noises from the teams or crowds. Solo sports also don't necessarily require the motor skills some Aspergers are known to struggle with, like eye-hand coordination and the timing and planning of movements. Solo sports give the Aspie confidence, allowing her to practice and improve on her own schedule, essentially being her only competitor, whose last record must be broken. An Asperger who wishes to try a few solo sports could choose from activities like jogging, running, cycling, swimming, golf, weight lifting and martial arts.

If there's a way to describe how an Aspie's athletic abilities can flourish in a solo setting, one could definitely look at Forrest Gump. Gump wasn't a skilled athlete but could run faster than an Aspie does to get away from relatives at a family reunion. The movie was based on a novel by the same name, but Gump's character was changed quite a bit by the time he made it to the screen. Interestingly, while the movie portrays him as having simple abilities, Winston Groom's book had him as one with above average autistic savant abilities, receiving a perfect score on an advanced physics exam.

Moving to or Staying in a Foreign Country

An Asperger with an interest in foreign relations who also wants to hide his social clumsiness may opt to move to or stay for extended periods in a foreign country.

People in other cultures will easily forgive an Asperger's awkward moments, attributing it to not being brought up in the culture. Some especially forgiving and loving people in some wonderful cultures will continue to do so years after the Asperger has been living there and should really be acting normal by that time. Or they will just, in the polite social manner that the people of the culture do, smile to his face but laugh behind his face.

To get into a foreign country, you need more than a VISA. You need a purpose for getting there. So, as college students, Aspergers should plan accordingly and take business classes in foreign relations. They should take advantage of programs abroad for as many summers and semesters as it takes to find out which country is either 1. Best suited for their tastes or 2. Has people who are most likely to put up with them.

Accepting any job where traveling abroad is required is not only a great way to get your foot in the door, but into another world as well.

Fiction

As adolescents, Aspie girls may develop an intense fondness for old, dead men.

No, she hasn't taken a liking to making stops at the local morgue to get a date for turnabout, she simply can't get enough of Shakespeare, Browning, Keats and other writers of classic literature.

It's been noted that many Aspergers hate fiction. That's true. But they also love fiction. This isn't meant to confuse you. There are plenty of other Asperger behaviors that will do that. Fiction is, once again, one more paradox for an Asperger. While it's true that one of the criteria for evaluating the adult Asperger is the dislike of fiction, for some Aspies, fiction is actually loved so much, it's the special interest.

An interest in fiction doesn't have to lead to any greater interest in academia, such as majoring in literature. But it would be cool to become an instructor of literature or an English teacher and do nothing but discuss this special interest day in and day out.

During 10th grade English, the fiction loving Aspie can sit back and dive into the fantasies of young lovers and the discussions of themes in *Romeo and Juliet*. Sitting in the same room, her logical, left-brained Asperger classmate is pulling her hair out in nothing but contempt because she is unable to grasp the irrational behavior between two teenagers she feels should have just 1. Waited until they were emancipated before embarking on a relationship and 2. Gotten a mediator involved to settle the dispute. (This same mediator could have also handled the emancipation papers, by the way.)

Computers

If it isn't already included in a list of traits to recognize when examining an individual for Asperger's, someone should officially put an interest in computers on every book of diagnostics on the shelves. Aspies are to computers like fish are to water. Often starting at an early age, the Aspie will learn and even teach herself every aspect of computers she can get her hands on. This interest may lead to anything from being an expert at the latest versions of every software released to computer programming to designing applications to physically building computers.

In ancient times, say when computers were as big as furnaces, IT guys were the dregs of corporate society with poor clothing taste, bad breath, bad communication skills and who's mere appearance at the office drove employees away from their cubicles in fear of catching nerd-disease.

Since the original settlers have continued to procreate and prosper in Silicon Valley, things have changed, and computer geeks are now the attractive technosexuals who've brought everyone, computer savvy or not, valuable tech software and platforms that have touched and improved their lives.

Pop culture has further elevated computer geeks into stardom from those entertaining Geek Squad dudes from the Best Buy commercials, the "Dell Dude" and the *Chuck* series characters.

It's often been said that IT has a higher percentage of Asperger individuals than other industries. The positive way tech nerds are being portrayed in today's world has resulted in one big bonus for the Asperger: an ever expanding little black book of women's numbers he only keeps in electronic form, backed up and saved on multiple drives that are also accessible via the most enhanced Wi-Fi capability. True, many of these numbers are from women who call him to remove a virus from their desktops, but some are from those that can't get enough of his big... joystick during weekend rendezvous.

An Asperger may even own multiple computers, as if he has several "pets," each having their specific uses for certain times. He or she is likely to be able to give advice on a wide range of tech topics to many people on a variety of technological levels. And more often than not, he or she will always be the one to fix a problem or teach friends and family the ins and outs of their computer.

J.F. Browne

Technosexuality

Does touching your iPod Touch arouse you as much as touching your partner or yourself?

Is your idea of "re-kindling" the romance in a relationship up-grading your Amazon Kindle?

During an erotic moment, when asked, "Where would you like to stick it?" do you automatically answer, "En gadget (.com)"?

If you answered, "yes," to any of these questions, you could be, like many Aspies, a technosexual.

In the risk of using a cliché, Aspergers often take to technology like a fish to water. Aspies not only embrace the world of tech, it's often a necessity for them to function on a regular basis and often becomes a source of income as many are found in the industry.

Even those on the Aspie continuum who are not found in highly technical fields find themselves practicing technosexuality every day. An Aspie may prefer tech items for gifts and spend her free time learning about the latest gadgets and educating herself on nerdy matters like how barcodes came to be on popular tech culture sites like *gizmodo.com* and learn who's who in the latest news of gadget inventors on places like *techcrunch.com*.

Wrong Planet

Talk to some Aspergers and you might find yourself wondering if these people are from completely different planets than the rest of the population. It's okay, because they usually don't mind this distinction and several thousand of these little Aspie aliens have joined together and regularly socialize, debate, get informed and just enjoy life with others from the same homeland on a website founded by an Asperger called Wrong Planet, at *wrongplanet.net*.

Wrong Planet is THE online hub for Aspergers. It has registered more than 50,000 members, with third-party web tracking services reporting over 400,000 total visitors to the site every month as of 2017. Keeping the extremely private Aspies happy, members can sign up with unique usernames and use avatars of their choice vs. a real photo. Wrong Planet was founded by Alex Plank, a graduate of George Mason University, who started the site not long after he was diagnosed with Asperger's.

In addition to its forum where members can start and respond to threads, Wrong Planet has a chat room, blog, news articles, interviews with famous Aspies like *America's Next Top Model* (cycle 9) contestant Heather Kuzmich and even an online shop to purchase Wrong Planet paraphernalia displaying the site's signature green alien. For humans, Wrong Planet has sold short and long-sleeved t-shirts, hats and caps, mousepads, wall clocks, mugs and tote bags. For pets, Wrong Planet has sold dog t-shirts. Recent visits showed no cat clothing was available. Which is probably good, given most of them have Asperger's and would probably squirm and throw a fit once they experienced the sensation of a human trying to dress them, giving them the urge to give their owner a sensory experience like no other via a paw full of sharpened claws.

For something originating from a different area in space, Wrong Planet sure has gotten a lot of good media attention here on Earth. It's been written about and mentioned by *New York* magazine, *Chicago Tribune* and *The Washington Post*. It's also been placed on the syllabus for classes at prestigious universities like Massachusetts Institute of Technology (MIT).

Wrong Planet serves as a good example of how Aspergers like to get together to spend time with people—sharing similar interests and making education, discussion and thought the themes of the event. Aspergers may have their deficiencies, but with over 50,000 registered friends, no one can ever argue that, among Wrong Planet users, a social life is one of them.

Foreign Language

The social language may be hard for the Asperger to grasp, but for many Aspies, it's the only one that doesn't come naturally.

Foreign language is sometimes a special interest for Aspergers. And it's often not just a passing phase that leaves most college students miserable several early mornings a week, forcing them to practice Cinco de Mayo every week by starting the day off with a margarita in order to tolerate the in-class exercises designed to help them distinguish between the use of "tu," "usted" and conjugate more than their share of "ar" and "er" verbs in one tense too many.

No, Aspergers would never use Google Translate to cheat with their homework assignments, not just because Google Translate often gives one effed up of an incorrect translation, but because there is no greater joy for these Aspies than to hammer through it with their knowledge.

Aspies don't stop at one language. They are often able to learn to read and speak several, sometimes very fluently. One of the biggest differences between an Asperger and a neurotypical who learns a foreign language is the Asperger can actually speak the language with little grammatical and other mistakes. This means the Asperger probably won't say things like, "I'll stick my foot in your anus manana," when she's trying to say, "Tomorrow I'll go shoe shopping with you."

The ability to get a foreign language to a T probably has something to do with the Aspie's ability to imitate—in this case, the exact accent of the natives in the country who speak the same language. It unfairly puts him first in line for future careers involving foreign speech, such as a translator.

And, if nothing else, makes it easier to nab a hottie foreign exchange student or someone from another country he will eventually marry.

Obsessions

An obsession can be a wonderful thing, so long as it's not an over-ly-priced bottle of cologne promoted by Calvin and his entourage of scantily clad models and other naked people that's so strong it even attracts the affection of four-legged wild animals.

Asperger obsessions tend to be just as strong as the cologne marketed by naked people in magazine ads and while occasionally cause some problems, are usually strong interests that are good to nurture, explore and can sometimes turn into a profitable venture.

Aspie obsessions are sometimes special interests and can in-volve a wide variety of subjects such as animals, plants, sports, sci-ence and tech. Unlike some OCD obsessions that are distressing to people, Aspie obsessions (unless they're OCD ones) are welcomed and pleasurable. They can be lifelong interests that are contin-uously fostered and developed or short-term fascinations that everyone around the Asperger can't wait to end so they can stop hearing about them. Which leads to another topic. Some potential obsessions—like Justin Bieber fever—are equally shared by neu-rotypicals and can be discussed freely among many people. Other obsessions, like colonies of bacteria found on common household items, are not as likely to win the Asperger points from the dinner crowd.

An MTV video featuring a hit song from the 1990s band Nelson may spark an obsession with its members. After CDs are bought, lyrics are studied, and live performances are attended, much time may be spent researching and learning how they come from several generations of successful musicians. These family members then become sub-obsessions. Suddenly, it becomes a priority to watch every old episode of *The Adventures of Ozzie and Harriet* before proceeding to study the films their equally famous sister Tracy starred in. This obsession will end once the Asperger decides the Nelson twins aren't nearly as interesting since they cut their long, beautiful, flowing blonde hair. Yeah, something about that Delilah effect makes Samson lose both his strength and fans.

Special Interests

If you happen to be in the company of the Asperger and he or she has not yet told you about their "special interest," it won't be long before you find out. And once they start talking, they will never shut-up about it.

Special interests usually fall under one of two categories: 1). collecting facts, which is often explained by experts as having an "encyclopedic knowledge," or never-ending or overflowing cup of information about a specific topic or 2). collecting objects or having a never-ending or overflowing room of items your roommate, spouse or mother desperately wants to put in a garage sale. Special interests can be about anything and range from computers to history to sports facts to science to animals to you name it. These interests make the Asperger proud of who he is ("I have the greatest stamp collection."), put her in a state of relaxation ("British music is the panacea for all woes.") and are much more intense than the hobbies of neurotypicals (think hiring a contractor to create space for your own National Geographic Library at home vs. owning a DVD copy of *Big Cats of the Jungle*). The special interest often develops at an early age and the Asperger has devoted lots of time reading, researching, collecting or doing whatever it takes to learn more about the topic. He or she has also taken turns driving various individuals nuts talking about the special interest—from family to teachers to friends and even total strangers who don't have the audacity to walk away.

It's important that the Asperger create an environment where the special interest can be pursued. This includes making a strong presence at family meetings where vacations are discussed so he or she can ensure the family is visiting a city which includes museums, shops and other places where the special interest can be fostered.

The urge to chase the special interest can pop up anywhere. If a husband and wife are sitting at the dinner table with [insert important person like boss or in-law], the following conversation might take place:

Asperger Spouse: Hey, ___, can I use your computer for a minute?

Host: Sure, it's right over in the other room. Forget to send some emails to the co-workers before you left work?

Asperger Spouse: (looking at watch) No, I've only got 15 minutes left to bid on a rare CD on eBay! (The rare CD being part of her music collection of 1000s.)

Note: Although this might incite a dirty and embarrassed look from the neurotypical spouse, the pursuit of the special interest will not be hindered provided the host has paid the Internet bill and the cat isn't sitting on the computer.

Big life decisions must be planned around the special interest. When looking to buy a home, the Aspie is faced with tough choices. Pay more for the model with the 2-car garage so that one garage can be used to store items related to the special interest? Although they have two children, the 4-bedroom home ensures the toy figurines from the Asperger's collection will be more comfortable in their own bedroom vs. a "small closet in the hallway." If the couple is "accidentally blessed" with another child...well... children should learn to share now, shouldn't they?

Facts and Trivia

Aspergers love facts and trivia. Many times, acquiring facts is also the special interest the Asperger has spent countless hours learning about. Like the special interest, the facts the Asperger retains could be about many things, including animals, science, technology, literature and so forth.

One of the reasons Aspergers love facts so much is because, unlike the rules of other parts of the neurotypical world such as facial expressions and implied meanings, facts are hard-and-fast, black and white and much easier to grasp. They are a sure thing to cling to in a world where the Asperger constantly must guess whether Heather really meant what she said when she said, "I never want to see you again," since she's said it so many times before calling to profess her undying love 48 hours later.

Facts and trivia can be a way to impress fellow nerds, geeks and Aspergers at the latest science fiction convention where a social structure might exist and the "Alpha Geek" is always the one who has the most facts to throw into the conversation.

They also provide reassurance and security. Let's say Joe is going over to Bill's house. Bill is a slob who cleans 1x a year maybe, leaves 2-month old dishes on the counter and whose vacuum serves more as a statue in the living room—the kind of expensive statue that obviously sets off alarms when you move it or he would have used it by now. "It's okay," thinks Joe, recalling the facts he learned from Immunology. "The skin is the largest organ in the body which provides the 1st line of protection against microbes. My skin will protect me from Bill's plague, and if not, there are plenty of NK cells and other white blood cells that will ward off any illnesses."

Occasionally, facts can be used as defenses and to re-establish superiority. Jenna's catty friend casually mentions that Jenna has wide hips. Jenna responds by recalling that studies show women with fuller thighs and hips, but small waists have better lipid profiles and have more intelligent babies. Depending on how much she values the friendship, she might go as far as to add that by comparing their two hips, her children will definitely be intellectually superior and will probably end up working for hers one day. For neurotypical translation, that's Asperger language for Jenna calling the catty friend a "bitch."

Non-Fiction and the Hatred of Fiction

The Asperger would prefer to read non-fiction books, unless the fiction books are based on real life events such as biographies or history. Aside from the ones that find literature to be a special interest, most Aspergers find fiction slow and boring; with all of its adjectives and phrases describing scenery and conversation that never took place to begin with. The Asperger would much rather read facts or other useful information that could be put to good use.

CliffsNotes were probably invented by an Asperger for the Asperger and they worked wonders until one 10th grade teacher announced that he would design questions on the test that could not be answered by reading the CliffsNotes alone.

"Who cares what Ken Kesey meant when he wrote, *One Flew Over the Cuckoo's Nest?*" thinks the Asperger. "Wasn't he doing LSD when he wrote that anyway? And how could anyone possibly write something that is worth my time analyzing and writing a paper on if they are clearly stoned?" (Note: The fact that the writer may have been stoned probably didn't sit too well with the Asperger either due to the Asperger's strong sense of morality.)

Fahrenheit 451 may have scored well on the Asperger's list of favorite books read in secondary school because it dealt with the idea of people losing interest in ridiculous literature and fantastic useful facts like what temperature it took to burn these ridiculous works. Some Aspergers find plays to be not as painful as at least some entertaining conversation takes place as opposed to paragraph upon paragraph of descriptions of brick streets, cottage houses and the shapes the clouds were making (or at least the shapes the stoner writer thought they were making) that day.

VI.

Education and Learning

Graduate School

Do you prefer high levels of psychological pain and torture? Are you looking to live in poverty for years? Do you find no greater pleasure than reading 1000s of articles on one specific protein that no one else cares about? If you answered, "yes," to any of the above questions, then there is a place for you that can only be compared to a combination of heaven and an amusement park.

That place is graduate school, which is a perfect setting for an Aspie who loves intellectual pursuits as it involves shunning oneself from the rest of the world, engaging immensely in the special interest and repetitively performing the same experiments over and over again in OCD-like fashion.

Many Aspergers who attend college see graduate school as a natural extension—the next step on the path to becoming a lifelong learner. Though seen as an academic pursuit, Aspergers also find graduate school a great place to practice their Asperger snobbery. This is accomplished by forming close associations with people who enjoy sitting in coffee shops and out fact-talking each other about the same protein. Maybe even taking turns reading to each other about the single protein during hard-core, party events like journal clubs.

In the end, there may be the possibility of landing a job in academia and forcing people to at least pretend to be interested in the same facts you can't get enough of because you can threaten their ~~futures~~ transcripts if they don't. And if not, at least you get the pleasure of attaching the designation of "Dr." in front of your name and following it with some sort of phrase indicating you are an "expert" in your field of special interest.

Self-Teaching

Give an Asperger the choice between a private tutor in the form of an expert human being and a CD and book tutorial on a subject and she'll gladly choose to watch boring slides on the computer.

Aspies are creatures of self-teaching and most begin this habit at an early age and continue into old age as they become lifelong learners. Aspergers begin by teaching themselves basic needed skills, such as basic computer skills, and may then progress to areas that are either of interest to them personally such as music or of necessity, such as career development. The self-teaching may also involve personal challenges or goals the Aspie regularly sets for himself. For example, one year, the challenge may be to learn basic French and the next to have a successful garden. The Asperger gets joy from playing Mr./Ms. Fix-It for problems others would readily call a help desk or repair person for.

As a child, the Aspie either amazed or drove his parents nuts taking things apart and (hopefully) successfully putting them back together just for the pure pleasure of learning how parts fit and how machines worked.

Instead of paying attention in class (or, when they were old enough to ditch class), the Aspie may have preferred to do other things like read a book or work on other schoolwork. It was then the Aspie learned the value of at least pretending to like socializing enough to talk to a few people he trusted to take good notes he could later copy. As technology advanced (and hopefully, the boring instructors), the Aspie could use the Internet to retrieve a nice, printed set of notes to refer to. The Asperger may have found it was actually easier to learn something by not going to class and listening to the teacher and just learning from the notes or reading the chapters.

Online Asperger Quizzes

The world of online quizzes can be an exciting and introspective place for one to learn about oneself. With hundreds of sites of-fering dozens and hundreds of quizzes, the path of enlightenment reaches as far as you can pick up your neighbor's unsecured Wi-Fi signal to stay online to take them.

Online quizzes fool idiots into thinking they have high IQs. Who doesn't want to know what kind of animal they are?

And last, but definitely not least, the online world is also a place for those interested in learning about Asperger's.

Whether you are Asperger, Asperger-curious (which disturb-ingly sounds like a quiz from some shady, online dating site), friend or family of Asperger, online quizzes provide a convenient, safe way to assess yourself or someone else and gather evidence to show to some potentially dull neurotypical who charges lots of money for you to sit on their cheap, tacky couch to tell you or someone you know really isn't Asperger, but instead are diagnosed with a popular term that's treated with the name of the medication on the oversized pen the pharmaceutical rep with the too short skirt brought him dozens of last week.

These quizzes will generally ask questions about a person's social, cognitive, sensory and communication experiences. Ones written by professionals that will likely get the neurotypical doctor you visit to put down his druggie pen and pay attention include the adult autism-spectrum quotient or AQ, a test developed by psychologist Simon Baron-Cohen and colleagues at the University of Cambridge's Autism Research Centre. Or the Australian Scale for Asperger's syndrome, a version for children.

And there's always the "What Kind of Asperger Animal are You?" quiz, which at least lets you know if you are a cat whose special interest is backyard squirrels or the dog whose collection compulsions include the neighbors' panties from their backyards during laundry days.

VII.

Sensory Issues

Sunglasses

Unlike the cheesy, '80s hit wonder, Canadian boy with the last name of Hart who crooned about wearing his sunglasses at night, most people wouldn't contemplate doing so.

However, Aspergers may wear their sunglasses at night, during a cloudy day, while driving during the day, inside a room with yucky fluorescent lights or while in front of a glaring computer monitor.

Due to sensory issues, bright light is a pain in the ass eye for the Asperger, sometimes literally.

As children, their mothers may have rushed them to the eye doctor after noticing they never turned on the light or lamp while reading or doing homework. After the eye doctor assured them that some people only need a little light to read, the mother sighed with relief, scratched off vision as the cause of her kid's other 200 eccentric behaviors and began thumbing through the yellow pages to consult with other professionals.

Sunglasses are as vital to the Asperger as earplugs. In many cases, leaving home without their shades is like leaving home without pants. Since sunglasses may be an integral part of an Aspie's life, he/she may want to invest considerable time in choosing the right pair. Unless they're prone to losing them often. In that case, perhaps collecting sunglasses as the special interest should be adopted, so they will never be without a pair.

Besides some of our society's awesomely famed blind individuals like musicians Stevie Wonder and Jeff Healey, the sunglass-wearing Asperger can be proud to share a fashion trend with many other notables who choose to go incognito for whatever reason. German fashion designer Karl Lagerfeld is rarely photographed without his. And who could blame him? After years of looking at what Anna Wintour throws together for *Vogue*, you'd cover your eyes too.

So, wear them proud, wear them anywhere and even wear your sunglasses at night. Except while driving, of course.

Touching and Not Touching—The Touchphillic and the Touchphobic

When it comes to touching, Aspergers fall into two categories: touchphillic and touchphobic. Some may be very comfortable with touching and even welcome it more than usual while others wished they really were the bubble boy everyone at school teased because they were sick so often—and literally enclosed in a bubble to prevent catching more germs.

While in some cultures people touch extensively in everyday interactions, such as kissing when meeting and holding hands when walking, for the most part, extreme touchy events don't happen during the 9-5 workday unless you're a woman taking the subway in New York or any other major metropolitan where the pervs have the same schedule as you do. Touchy moments are usually reserved for families during their quality time together (hugs, kisses and, "How was your day?") and romantic encounters between couples. This is where the tricky part comes for touchphobics, especially when they have a neurotypical partner who enjoys many displays of affection.

Both touchphobics and touchphillics experience sensory sensitivity to touch, but touchphillics thrive on it. The heightened experience is more enjoyable and may make them habitual gropers (consensual, not the kind on the subway), covering their partner's body as if they possessed eight octopus legs. They expect to be octopus-groped excessively as well. But most humans have only two arms and two legs, so this craving is never satisfied unless there's something freaky going on behind closed doors. Touchphobics, on the other hand, may feel uncomfortable with touch and not even engage in less arousing and more general affectionate behaviors like hand holding, arm touching and hugging outside of some contract forced upon them by the neurotypical partner who feels rejected for her octopus desires.

There is one possible solution, however radical it sounds. The full body condom.

Pushing Daisies was an American comedy-drama series that ran from 2007-2010. It featured a man named Ned who was given the ability to bring people back from the dead for a few seconds by touching them. When he touched them again, the person returned to death. If Ned waited too long before touching them again and putting them back to death, the consequence was another person alive died.

Ned accidentally leaves his childhood sweetheart Charlotte "Chuck" Charles alive and falls instantly back in love. But there's one problem (except for that poor dead person that had to go because Chuck stayed alive). He will never be able to even get to first base because of his touch of death. So, during one episode, the two figure out how to combat this by wearing full body suits that are a cross between a see-through hazmat suit and a space suit. Now they can touch (with their body condoms on) all they want, and Chuck won't die.

Of course, this isn't as practical for the couple with a touchphobic Asperger. For one, the plastic suits are most likely hot (and not the sexy kind of hot either). And bulky, meaning some of those insecure touchphobics will ultimately use the excuse to avoid sexy time by saying they look fat and feel unattractive in their plastic suit.

Survival Kits

The Scouts have the motto of always being prepared, so why shouldn't Aspergers do the same?

For some Aspies, there is a survival kit that's just as essential as water purification tablets, matches and a compass. The Asperger Survival Kit contains all the equipment an Aspie needs to navigate and survive the wilderness of the neurotypical world. It's a tough job, but at the end of the day, if the Aspie is well prepared, he finds his way back to the cabin unscathed.

The survival kit usually contains tools needed to combat sensory sensitivity issues, items that protect the senses. So, sunglasses for bright lights and earplugs for disturbing noises are likely included.

A creative entrepreneur should take the Asperger Survival Kit and really market it, seeing profits soar. Along with the Basic Survival Kit, there could be several lines designed to assist Aspies with unique needs. For the visually sensitive, the kit could contain several versions of sunglasses, perhaps with switch and swap features much like cell phones have different faces. And maybe darker outdoor shades vs. lighter indoor shades to accommodate for bright sunlight vs. annoying fluorescent lights. Light earplugs for indoor events such as the classroom and test taking and situations where you still need to hear what's going on around you. And heavy-duty earplugs for the times you're dragged to the VIP section of metal concerts by your friends.

Years from now, when you're watching an infomercial at 2:00 a.m. for multiple Asperger Survival Kits that can be purchased with "3 easy payments" on your credit card...remember you heard it here first.

Earplugs

All humans, neurotypical or Asperger, have their "I can't do without" accessories. Belts, bracelets, push-up bras, you name it. Most of these accessories are for vanity purposes and the person could very well tolerate being separated from, although they might suffer extreme feelings of ugliness, nakedness, fattiness, skinniness, [insert negative psychological feeling of materialistic, neurotic individual].

The Asperger has an accessory, but unlike most neurotypical accessories, it is, for some, an absolute necessity. That accessory is the pair of earplugs.

Many Aspergers have various sensory sensitivities, meaning certain sensory stimuli like noises, smells, lighting, tastes and touches are more overwhelming for them than for most neurotypicals and can sometimes hinder performance or just make life annoying. One of the ways the clever Asperger has learned to circumvent this sensitivity is by following the Scouts' motto and being prepared by keeping a set of earplugs with them at all times.

This preparation comes in handy to drown out a noisy subway; when you are dragged to a loud concert by a spouse or at least someone you might want to con into being your spouse one day; a library that isn't always as quiet as it should be; screaming ungrateful brats that share your DNA (that you're 99.9% sure of according to that test); the wife that talks too much in the car and the various sounds of papers turning, pens and pencils scribbling and people moving up and down in squeaky chairs during important tests. In some cases, such as taking standardized tests at some official centers, the neurotypicals have evolved and learned that many people can benefit from such measures and provide free earplugs to testers. These drown out such nuisances as keyboard typing or loud gas from the nervous dude next to you. Most times, however, the Asperger is on his own.

There are times when the Asperger may be extremely stressed and feel the need to wear the earplugs for longer periods of time and to more places such as the few last days before a big project that requires constant thinking and concentration. Many people who know the Asperger have learned when these times exist and may accommodate: Suzy is wearing her earplugs while she washes dishes. I won't bother her for now. I'll wait until she talks to me.

Sometimes, these periods of earplug wearing may go on and on and people around the Asperger, such as the neurotypical significant other, may start to wonder when this "period" will subside and they will be able to communicate with the Asperger again. Although there is no known exact formula to predict this, much data exist that shows one strong correlation: when the feud between the wife and her (sister/mother/boss/friend) has ended and she no longer has the need to tell you every detail night after night, the sensory sensitivity period magically (no, abruptly, with magically being a bad scientific word) ceases, thus providing a supportive environment for the earplugs to come out.

Nakedness

Clothing can be such a pain in the ass for Asperger people. Too tight, not tight enough, feels scratchy, the list goes on for material and fabrics that rub their sensory sensitivities the wrong way.

Because of this, some Aspergers prefer to go plain naked.

Usually this is confined to a private area, such as one's own home or apartment, but there are exceptions.

As children, they may be little "streaker tykes," taking off clothing that is unbearable in any environment, including public places. Some adult Aspergers may still take their clothes off in public, depending on their level of fitness and audacity and the amount of money offered that has enticed them to do so.

Nakedness is natural and fine, but Aspergers must beware: Google is watching.

Google Maps is a lovely application that allows you to ~~stalk~~ view a detailed map of many areas, from the street signs of an intersection all the way down to the color of the mailbox in front of a person's home. Because of this, being naked in the backyard, even with a privacy fence, comes with the risk of you exhibiting yourself on Google Maps.

What's more, one blogger reported that Google Maps was able to focus the camera so closely, it caught her cat in the window of the living room. And that cat wasn't even naked.

This could only mean one of two things: 1. Google likes to look at naked people. 2. Google likes to look at naked Asperger people, knowing Aspergers like to get naked.

It is probably a combination of both.

So be free, be naked, but don't forget to close the opaque curtains.

VIII.

Morals, Principles and Values

Questioning Authority

In some ways, an Asperger having issues with authority seems almost paradoxical.

After all, Aspergers love rules, standards, protocols and all things that contain order.

But just like the Aspie has a need to know which rules are the right rules to follow, he/she desperately needs to feel the authority over him is the right person for the job. If not, they should be removed. How is this determined? By constantly questioning, arguing with and driving the authority to the point of no return by belittling their methods and suggesting how things could be done better.

As an adult, the Asperger must fight his urges to keep from lashing out verbally at a boss he deems too stupid to make the coffee, let alone give him a paycheck. Because the adult Asperger has spent years analyzing and has a pretty good idea of who and who not to pay attention to, he has no problem stating why Person X is the most moronic person in the world to take advice from (too ugly for makeup advice, too fat for diet advice, people from that town aren't very bright), albeit if only behind Person X's back.

If the authority figure possesses the patience (and the self-esteem) to withstand the Asperger's evaluation, he/she will be elevated as the person who earned the Asperger's coveted, rare respect. In most cases, this never happens, not because there aren't any good authority figures in the world, but because the Asperger cannot continue to evaluate if he/she is sent one too many times to the school counselor's office because the authority has deemed his/her constant evaluation to be disruptive to class and a pain in the butt.

The Asperger will devote a great deal of time questioning why the teacher is assigning certain assignments over others. The Asperger will have suggestions as to how to make the learning experience superior to that of the teacher's methods (e.g. instead of memorizing four dozen presidential names, why not write an essay comparing and contrasting two?)

The phrase "because I said so" is easy to translate into many languages. But there is no language in the world that can convince the Asperger to do something without you explaining why. And even if you explain why, there's no guarantee the Asperger will agree your reason is correct.

Once a person realizes it's just a matter of giving references when defending themselves to prove their rank to the Asperger, life will become much easier. After all, how hard could it be to offer 10 original articles on the benefits of beta carotene, explain how fiber aids in regularity and show two videos comparing organic vs. inorganic produce before getting your child to eat his ½ cup of carrots at dinnertime?

Doing Things Their Way

There's usually more than one way to solve a problem. There is the Asperger way to solve a problem. But when the Asperger uses his/her way, it's usually considered the only way, and they can be notorious for not seeking advice to solve problems and not considering, flat out laughing at the idea of doing things differently.

In school, we were taught certain ways to solve problems in analytical courses like mathematics. Credit was often given even for incorrect answers as long as steps involved in solving the problem were listed. This was sometimes an issue for the Asperger, as he may have figured out a unique way to solve it, and consistently loss points. Of course, as math problems got harder—possibly involving larger numbers—it became clear there was a good reason for using the formula the other 24 children in the class used that was derived from some old guy who got off looking at triangles and degrees all day long and decided to make up his way of doing them.

Solving problems their way may extend to social situations. Instead of getting advice from a friend or professional about relationship issues, the Asperger may try to figure things out for himself. This is why so many men buy their wives fantastically romantic gifts like solar powered hair removal tools for the 25th anniversary. *Wife's going through menopause*, Aspie thinks. *She's got facial hair now. This will help her get rid of it AND help the planet*. Between this tool and the gift certificate to the varicose vein specialist, Casanova will have the special weekend covered.

Being Right and Not Admitting They're Wrong

Consider these odds, each of which has a low probability to occur:

The odds of becoming a president

The odds of winning the lottery

The odds of becoming a saint

The odds of a meteorite landing on your home

The odds of some Aspergers admitting they're wrong: not officially calculated anywhere, but probably lower than all four of the above unlikely chances.

As people grow older, they develop mature, conflict-resolution tactics. When something isn't working, they admit to a mistake. Understand that it will take the Aspie longer than others to come around and do this. Understand that deep within the brain structure and psychological complexity of the Aspie, resides a god complex. God does not admit to making a mistake and if you force him to, he might just send a large meteorite down on your home. But he will probably just engage in a long argument with you, bringing up facts that kind of show he's right, but not really. But if he rambles off enough facts or makes enough counter arguments, he will attempt to wear you down psychologically, thus taking over your mind and making you think he's right. If this doesn't work, he'll just admit...that he's right.

Getting an Asperger to admit they're wrong is a tricky technique. If you can, well, congratulations to you, as you've just performed a miracle, increasing your chances of being canonized. For most others, they have a greater chance of some really cool rock from outer space hitting their home that they can later brag about and show to everyone at the next neighborhood association meeting where the Asperger neighbor down the street always reminds people to follow the strict rule of placing the garbage can 10 inches from the curb. For anyone unable to measure this distance on their own, he's happy to mark it on the concrete for them. The trash can rule is a hard-core fact, printed on paper, distributed to everyone and signed and enforced by the correct authorities who have earned their power over the neighborhood.

And darn it, this makes him right.

Strong Sense of Justice

Aspergers are known for having incredible senses of justice. They want to right rights and make the wrongs pay. This is why they readily tell on their friends who do bad things in class. Justice must be contagious because these ex-friends then feel the need to seek it and later do so by going after them during recess on the playground. Adolescent and young adult Aspies seek answers to injustices they feel are prevalent in society like civil rights and humanitarian issues. In these cases, the Aspie may feel certain people deserve more or better than what society makes accessible to them, such as quality of education, food or housing.

An Aspie often goes into deep thought about the slightest acts of injustice, which often ignite their critical and abrasive personalities. An Aspie may wonder in disgust why smokers in the workplace are allowed to go on as many breaks as they want to work towards killing themselves, but healthy employees aren't allowed to get up and take two-minute walks every one to two hours. Especially when it's been proven by researchers that sitting down for prolonged periods is bad for heart health and getting up and moving may prevent fatigue and blood clots. He may even think to himself (being careful not to say thoughts aloud as usual) that the boss who forbids breaks for non-nicotine addicts could stand to initiate a walking and exercising break movement for the entire department. This would especially benefit most of management, considering they're all diabetic with glaucoma and are always first

J.F. Browne

in line to get the company treats that are served at least three times a day.

Sometimes, while striving to determine what's right or appropriate, the Aspie goes overboard, reverting to the ancient rules for punishment, as in an "eye for an eye" mentality. This is especially convenient if the Aspie is the target of the injustice. The child Aspie may put deep thought into figuring out ways to repay a school bully or playmate that crossed him the wrong way. Or draft dozens of plans designed to "teach someone a lesson."

Adult Aspies teach lessons and channel their sense of justice in more appropriate and sometimes weird ways. It could include obtaining the telephone number of the owner of the car who almost crashed into the Aspie, due to many negligent factors, like talking on the cell phone or eating and trimming their toenails while making a left-hand turn. Then contacting them and giving them a firm lecture on cell phone usage while driving, along with an insult that their toes are quite ugly and should not be anywhere visible, such as on the dashboard where other drivers may see them. The Aspie may feel this call is best done at 4:00 a.m.—just to make sure it's the first call the driver receives before leaving that day, so he'll remember no texting and toe trimming while driving.

Aspergers Do It—And Demand You Do It Like Them

Aspergers do it...then demand you do it their way too.

Anyone who spends time with an Aspie may soon learn that Einstein was full of it and there is no such thing as relativity. At least when it comes to the correct way of doing things. At a certain age, most Aspergers become enlightened and reach the conclusion that there is only one, correct way of doing something. The exact age of that enlightenment is unknown, but most experts would agree it's, on average, just a few days after being released from utero.

Aspergers who want the best for everyone (or at least themselves), will not only ensure they do things the correct way, but go out of their way to ensure others do it their way—the correct way—too. Not adhering to their way of doing things results in anything from a mild tongue lashing to a speech on why their way is better to a full blown, "You're an idiot for not listening to me," diatribe.

Demanding you do it their way can expand into several areas of living, including, but not limited to the following: work and employment situations, money and finances, diet, personal relationships, raising children, raising pets and raising children of pets.

Family members living with an Asperger who adopts a new diet for weight loss will have plenty of opportunity to support him—because they now will be forced to only eat what he eats daily, even if there's no need to lose a few pounds.

Religion may be a haven for these Aspies, especially if they belong to one of the religions that believe what is best for the world is to annihilate everyone in every other religion that differs from their own. This could potentially include any religion. Except for some forms of Mormonism, of course. The frustrations of learning empathy and reciprocation with one partner is more than any Asperger man can handle. A multitude of partners would send him straight to his Asperger cave every evening reading to catch up on the latest news about his special interest of proving which version of the Bible should be taken literally.

Rules: Following, Enforcing and Rule Enforcement Pissiness

The Asperger is a lover of all rules. It is not enough to just follow them, in some cases, the Asperger feels he or she must create more rules and enforce rules on other people. Usually, the Asperger thinks he/she is doing the right thing because of their strong sense of morality and they can't see any other way of doing it because of their tendency to think in extremes. Some may be driven because of anxiety of breaking a social norm and desperately wanting to do what is proper.

Still, others suffer from R.E.P., otherwise known as Rule Enforcement Pissiness.

Rule Enforcement Pissiness can be explained by the following: Growing up and even as an adult, the Asperger learned that some of his/her behavior and mannerisms were not necessarily appropriate socially (staring hard at people that looked damn fine, telling them they are indeed, "too fat," and then saying, "You wanted to know."). People who cared for the Asperger's social development (and wanted to protect them from getting their asses kicked) constantly reminded the Asperger of what the social norms were and how to follow them. Eventually, most of them got this and were able to at least fake their way through life.

However, all this felt quite unnatural. Even worse, the Asperger had to observe neurotypical people getting away with breaking all the rules he was so chastised for not following: being rude, offensive, saying overtly sexual lines, grabbing...you get the point. "Screw this," the Asperger thought. "If I have to follow these weird social rules, then I'm going to make sure everyone does." And off on a mission the Asperger went to help enforce them, being seriously afflicted with R.E.P.

Great careers in administration, auditing and neighborhood association weirdo always seen carrying a yardstick to measure your grass blades were launched.

Before these careers, the Asperger had lots of practice in school. Reminding the teacher three minutes of class remained and students should not be dismissed. Telling the college professor, she shouldn't cancel class because there are X number of classes on the syllabus and students are paying for X number of classes. Maybe even going to the dean to complain.

It's important the Asperger realize it is not about themselves changing. They should continue living their lives according to their rules and it's probably healthier they do. This rule adherence is more than likely responsible for the Asperger achieving in areas they choose to pursue.

Not fatal, but downright annoying, R.E.P. can be alleviated once the Asperger learns that everything in life is not black and white. This can be accomplished by exposing the Asperger to different people and different environments, giving explanations of why things can have more than one solution. A four-year stint at a nice liberal arts university might help in this process as the Asperger can observe many people who have different rules and are either creating their own rules, changing rules or even downright disregarding them.

This will result in the Asperger realizing that yes, there are shades of gray. Either that or they will run off to join the priesthood/nunnery as reactive therapy.

Morals (The Right Ones, That Is)

Aspergers have spent many sleepless nights debating the morality of both their actions and others. They are naturally hyper-concerned with doing what is right, judging if others are doing what is right and ensuring others know what is right. Their innate strong sense of what's right and wrong has both protected and punished them throughout their lives.

On the positive side, an Asperger's strong sense of morality will ensure that Barbara Walters will never be able to write a tell-all book about him. Ditto for any Paris Hilton-like videos surfacing the Internet and time spent wasting away in Margaritaville. That itself should make him appreciative of this gift. But a closer look at the Asperger's conscience on overdrive reveals problems surfacing more than occasionally.

There is always the risk of offending a friend or potential girlfriend if she is told her outfit makes her look like a whore. But the Asperger feels compelled to tell her this anyway. After all, she may not know. And if she doesn't who else is going to tell her? Morals such as these must be followed even at the risk of a slap to the face or a knee to the groin.

College can be a time of great frustration for the Asperger when deciding on a major. A promising career as an attorney may sound exciting, but the Asperger cannot foresee giving a person without scruples counsel even if they deserve it. Medicine might prove lucrative and honorable, but if people can prevent so many ailments through diet and exercise it's not progressive to treat them with drugs. A librarian may seem like the perfect job as literacy and education can never be overpromoted. Until the Asperger imagines a situation where she is forced to tell a patron to be quiet only to discover the patron has a voice disorder that makes it difficult to do so. Because of her chastising the patron, the patron decides to become a recluse for 30 years and blames the Asperger librarian for driving him to a lifetime of isolation and cold delivered pizzas because he no longer feels confident leaving the home to go grocery shopping. While this scenario might sound farfetched, it seems quite plausible at 3:00 a.m. over nail biting and undergraduate class registration forms on the table.

The moral weight of responsibility the Asperger feels is often too much to carry. Because of this, some will stop this progressive, thought-provoking process and resort to easy, mindless thinking as a Rule Enforcement Pisser to compensate.

Honesty

Asperger people have an innate drive to be honest and truthful. If your best friend or partner is an Asperger, his or her straightforwardness can take the guesswork out of life, making time spent together simple, less stressful and more rewarding. It can also make things difficult.

Gas is expensive enough. There's nothing worse than your Asperger partner insisting on driving 50 miles back to the hotel to return an unused bar of soap accidentally taken. Ditto for the pen with the neat-looking logo. It all has to stay in Vegas, darn it. The Asperger child may be a parent's dream come true, as he will always tell on himself after being naughty. The same child may be looking for new friends after deciding it really is best to let the teacher know who prank called her home at 3:00 a.m. after she gives a lecture (albeit in between yawning) to the entire class on how it's important to speak up and do the right thing.

Preying can be a problem, as Aspergers freely give any information asked for, never believing anyone would use it against them or to harm them. A hard lesson can be learned from finding out your idea has been taken—word for word, step by step—for a class project or discovering your entire list of clients disappearing and going to that "other company" a "friend" happened to start after innocently offering to proofread business documents or install important updates to your software.

The Asperger employee may or may not be the "one" of the month when he blows the whistle hard enough for everyone in the overseas affiliate company to hear when the location of the missing file is revealed to be thrown in the trash bin that suddenly needs to be emptied ASAP. Due to an Asperger's strong urge to be truthful, it's important to plan ahead in terms of what profession to go into. While integrity is valued by most employers, there will be some jobs the Asperger person may have to look over.

The following are professions that an Asperger could consider which reward him or her for honesty:

Auditing

Clergy

On the contrary, some professions in which the Asperger's honesty might cause difficulties are:

Lawyer

Corporate Manager

Politician

Lawyer

Lawyer for the business where the corporate manager works

Lawyer for the politician who got caught doing something with the corporate manager after hours...

IX.

Emotions and the Touchy Feely

Staying Calm in Crazy Situations

When the crowded elevator gets stuck in the middle of a ride down from the 50th to the 1st floor and the pregnant woman's water has just broken, most people in the elevator would start to feel uneasy.

The Asperger is likely to not blink at the situation. He'll tell everyone to stay calm while he calls for help, remembering some obscure facts he read about home delivery on a random website in case he has to play doctor before the car hits the next floor.

He will carefully explain to the screaming woman in pain about his knowledge of childbirth and assure her she's in good hands. That doesn't mean she's letting him anywhere near her lady parts. But just in case, he's prepared.

For some reason, Aspergers are known for being able to stay calm in otherwise calamitous situations that send everyone else into panic attacks.

This may be because the Asperger is the king of figuring things out through reason and intellect, two things that normally disappear from neurotypicals when they're stressed. While neurotypicals are screaming hysterically, feeling faint and, in general, just losing it during stressful times, the Asperger will work to solve a problem through questioning and answering. Common questions may include:

What exactly is the issue?

Why is this happening?

What are the options (counting or listing) that I have to fix the problem?

What kind of time frame do I have for patching things up?

Have I seen or experienced something like this before and can I use a past experience or knowledge to solve this problem?

What resources do I have available?

The Asperger knows that pulling hair out, burying one's face in one's hands or having a nervous breakdown is never the answer to emergencies. Those antics are best saved for real disasters, like when the pancake shop is out of strawberry jam, forcing him to modify his breakfast order from the past 10 years and spread strawberry preserves on the waffle instead.

X.

Planning and Organizing

Planning and Appointments

Those needing to talk to or see an Asperger had better check his Outlook calendar before wandering into his cubicle, even if it's just for a 2-minute talk to see how he's doing. This probably isn't a good idea anyway unless mandated by management because he would never voluntarily accept an appointment for small talk, making the excuse he's completely booked, even when it's plain as day his public calendar is and has been open for months (because nobody *really* wants to have small talk with him).

Although some Aspergers struggle with planning and management, the ones that get it are savants at it. Every detail of life is accounted for through day (and night) planners, wall calendars, daily calendars, alarms, reminder notes and so forth.

These Aspies thrive on appointments in their lives and have a time set aside for each and every step taken. They will get angry if others don't adhere to the appointed times, but even angrier when there's an unannounced visit or something that deviates from the schedule.

If you ever show up at these Aspies' homes without calling, they might be so irate at your lack of respect for the "calendar," they might not answer the door for you. Even when it's clear they're home because you hear noise when you ring the doorbell or knock on the door. Or because the curtains and blinds are open. Or they live in one of those cool, sunroof-like homes with glass walls. Actually, since some Aspies prefer to go without clothes because of sensory issues, the last two are unlikely to happen. But still, you *know* they're home.

Perhaps the Aspie's extreme need for routine is what drives them to love the structured life. The unexpected is disturbing, stressful and just downright annoying. So always plan. Give her a call first. But if the matter is something uninspiring, boring or excessively social, don't be surprised if the call is magically "dropped" despite having a cell phone tower so close to you it looks like you're taking a tourist photo in front of the Eiffel.

J.F. Browne

Rehearsals

It's no secret that Aspergers love rehearsals. No, this doesn't mean they enjoy getting dressed up in uncomfortable attire and standing next to an annoying soon-to-be in law while watching and listening to even more annoying and soon-to-be brothers and sisters-in law bicker about their place in the lineup.

Being excellent actors, Aspergers will often spend much time rehearsing what they are going to do or say before executing the action in a social setting. This may be because they are forgetful, socially anxious and the repetition eases their anxiety or are not very experienced interacting verbally with many individuals.

Unless you count those verbal interactions with the cat.

The rehearsal sessions often include both verbal and non-verbal actions, and the hardest working Aspie actors will practice both what they are going to say and any facial expressions and/or hand gestures that fit well with his/her lines.

The rehearsing Aspie who loves to theorize and predict outcomes will create different statements and responses based on what she thinks the other person might say or do. An entire algorithm could be created based on the opposite person responding with statement A, B, C or D.

After creating the script, the Aspie needs someone to rehearse the social event in front of. The most obvious and best critic is himself in the mirror. But the Aspie is often always his worst critic so it's always best to get an opinion from a gentler reviewer.

Like the cat.

When the Asperger is finally performing the scene live (aka trying to convince the other person to do things their way or agree with them), a number of scenarios could take place. Some Aspies follow the script completely. Some improvise parts of it. Some toss the screenplay out altogether and wing it.

Over time, social interactions become easier and there's less need for practice. Which is a relief to the cat as it can now tend to more important matters—like licking its tail or being spooked by his own reflection in the mirror—than the Asperger's social rehearsals.

Making Lists

List making is one of the most preferred methods of organizing for Aspergers. The typical Asperger guy or gal may spend a lot of time making lists, lists of lists, list of when to make more lists, list of how to organize lists and so forth.

List making is one of the hallmark traits a neurotypical will give when describing their Asperger friend, family member or partner. Usually, this is done in a negative way—as if there is a problem with making lists.

Like many other traits the Asperger possesses that may irk his/her neurotypical company, list making is just another way the Asperger organizes his/her life and makes him/her so efficient at doing the things they do so well.

There may be a few times when list making is taken to the extreme. In an episode of *Seinfeld*, Jason Alexander's character George Constanza made a list he referred to as "Crib Notes." These hints, written in ink on his palm, gave George a handy cheat sheet to glance at while trying to impress a new romantic interest in bed. "Crib Notes," written on the hand (or anywhere else on the body) are NOT good lists, and any Asperger (or neurotypical for that matter) should avoid making these types of lists as much as possible.

Finally, if there was any evidence to show how good lists can be, we only have to look at one very powerful figure in biblical history. That's right, Moses. He took a simple list, 10 rules to live one's life by, and wrote this on a stone tablet. Granted, most people today rarely adhere to this list. However, this great organizer performed feats that most neurotypicals could only dream of doing.

So, the next time an Asperger is criticized about list making, he or she should ask a few questions about the naysayer: Can this person put up with people for 40 years in a hot desert? Are they able to separate seas? If list making puts the Asperger in the company of anyone who can do this, then it's certainly not a bad habit at all.

XI.

Pop Culture

Mental Floss

Mental Floss is a magazine with an online component *mentalfloss. com*, who's tagline says it all: *Where Knowledge Junkies Get Their Fix*.

Filled with nothing but articles, trivia, quizzes and briefs on every topic you could imagine, *Mental Floss* may be the hub where Aspies who speak Factanese can get their fix.

Nowhere but the "Quizzes" section can you test your ability to distinguish whether Ziro, Salporin, Yasmin and Jolessa are "Birth Control or *Star Wars* Characters?"

Some blog posts, like detailed explanations of how Dum Dums creates the "Mystery Flavor" of lollipop, is sure to win the crowd at your next dinner party.

Perhaps the most titillating component of online *Mental Floss* is "The Amazing Fact Generator." A brief description of a fact is shown on the screen (like the fact "dude" is used 161 times in the movie *The Big Lebowski*). To get another fact, simply press the "More Facts Please!" button. And more. And more. And more. Until you're so overcome knowing a "crash" is a group of rhinos, the name of a famous Italian pickle merchant or that there are GPS devices that can be installed in nativity scenes that, although won't help the wise men figure out where to deliver the next batch of gold, frankincense and myrrh, can prevent theft of Jesus during the Christmas season, allowing prostitutes like Mary Magdalene to escape the radar during this time of year. It is the perfect way to sublimate your desires to ramble about these things during work so that you ensure you won't drive co-workers nuts and continue to receive a steady paycheck to go towards purchasing those dolls you collect in the garage.

So which characters are *Star Wars* vs. birth control names? Ziro and Salporin would know Jabba the Hutt and Chewbacca, while Yasmin and Jolessa prevent the birth of a lightsaber.

Heather Kuzmich and Her Hot Legs

Heather Kuzmich is one well-known Asperger who many consider to be of importance in the culture. She was a contestant on *America's Next Top Model* (cycle 9) series where she made it to the final five.

Kuzmich is appreciated, revered and adored by Aspergers for several reasons. One, she brought Asperger's to the limelight on a national television show watched by many neurotypicals who were not previously educated on the topic or the individuals. She also showed that women and girls can be Aspergers too, shattering the stereotype that it's just a male thing. Because of this, possibly more gals will realize they are Aspergers or stop covering up their Asperger traits just because they can fake it better than dudes. Clinicians might wise up and recognize girl Aspergers, correctly informing them and giving them the insight they need to move forward in life. But as any Asperger who has dealt with those types of neurotypicals knows...some dull pencils in the box are harder to sharpen than others.

Kuzmich came across as intelligent, articulate and well-adjusted. She also had a great pair of legs.

And what fantasies both neurotypical and Asperger men held to procreate with her and produce their very own Asperger mini-mes, fascinating and entertaining with their abilities to talk for hours about special interests like animals, nature, art and computers, navigating through and dominating life with their superior logic and analytical skills and turning heads everywhere with their hot pairs of legs.

Although her tenure on *America's Next Top Model* didn't result in a victory, she gained fame, respect, other modeling opportunities and proved she and other Aspergers, can not only have hot legs, but can compete with any regularly wired individual.

Dropping Bill Gate's Name to Honor Their Aspergerness

When discussing Asperger people, some have used Bill Gates as an example of someone who possesses Asperger traits. Although it's not officially known if Gates is an Asperger or not, his nerdy brilliance, computer knowledge and skills, intense focus in a particular narrow field or "special interest" and his blunt, abrasive statements to people like, according to articles from both *wired. com* and *time.com*, "Have you ever tried thinking?" and, "That's the stupidest thing I've ever heard," certainly make him a potential candidate.

Aspergers across the universe know this and will use this suggestion to honor and defend their "Aspergerness" at any given time they feel "Asperger" is being used in a derogatory manner.

"Bill Gates probably has Asperger's."

"Asperger's is good. Isolated focus is what made Bill Gates a zigazillionaire."

"Asperger's is a gift. Without it, we wouldn't have people like Bill Gates."

You see the point by now.

Asperger traits, however, can be both good and bad, and many Aspergers have started to drop his name to defend their negative "Aspergerties (unofficial name for traits associated with Asperger's)."

"Why can't I grab and adjust myself at the dinner party? It's part of my Aspergerness and I'm sure Bill Gates would grab and scratch himself at any dinner party if he felt the urge."

"Why help my wife put away groceries? If she knows how to buy them, she ought to know how to put them away. I've got programming to do. Would Bill help Melinda put away the groceries?"

Fanatic followers of Bill Gates name dropping take on the WWBG motto: What would Bill Gates do? Usually the answer is that Bill Gates would do the opposite of what the Asperger is trying to avoid doing.

Most Bill Gates name droppers are computer geniuses (albeit self-professed), but the expertise of these followers can vary. Some will drop his name even though they think "Vista" is a vocabulary word from Spanish Level 1 and "XP" is a dress size you wear for a month after gluttonous holiday eating.

Cameron, an Asperger-Like Robot from *Terminator: The Sarah Connor Chronicles*

Terminator: The Sarah Connor Chronicles was a popular television series that aired on Fox between 2008 and 2009. In 2011, the Syfy channel gained the rights to air all 31 of the episodes. This sci-fi drama features a robot named Cameron that displays many Asperger traits. The whole gist of the story is this: Sarah Connor (Lena Headey) has a son, John (Thomas Dekker). John is being pursued by Terminators that want to destroy him because John is so special he has been chosen to save mankind from destruction by machines. They recruit Cameron, a Terminator played by actress Summer Glau, who has been reprogrammed to help instead of hurt John and off they go running from the Terminators, trying to figure out how to stop them. In between plots, there are love stories, adolescent angst and plenty of robots getting blown up, shredded, burned and then putting themselves back together before reactivating and chasing after John again. Pretty typical life for a teenage boy.

Cameron follows John wherever he goes, including school. Although she is beautiful, it's not long before John and everyone else who interacts with her realizes that she is a little bit "different," causing her to lose some points in the congeniality area with her peers. She is supposed to be able to blend in and interact with real humans better than the other robots, but she has her moments.

The following are a few examples:

A. Asperger Trait: Telling the truth with brutal honesty without taking into consideration the feelings of others.

Scenario: High school bathroom with lots of teenage girls. One girl asks Cameron if she looks fat in an outfit. Cameron says of course she does. Her reply results in a string of profanities from the girl seeking advice. Obviously surprised by the girl's anger, Cameron reminds her, "You asked."

B. Asperger Trait: Literal interpretation or misinterpretation of phrases/not understanding pop culture or slang phrases.

Scenario: Sarah, John and Cameron are all getting into a vehicle. "I call shotgun," John says while getting in the front passenger seat. To which Cameron says, "I call nine millimeter." Which is probably what she'll use to disable a Terminator within the next 10 minutes of the scene.

C. Asperger Trait: Using appropriate social skills or phrases, but not doing so smoothly. Timing is off, phrasing is somewhat incorrect, or the social skill displayed is the right mannerism at the wrong time.

Scenario 1: Cameron is conducting a bank heist to access a special vault that will take them to another time. "Everybody on the ground," she yells, brandishing a firearm. But remembering her programmed manners, she follows it up with (after a brief pause), "Please."

Scenario 2: Picks up a small boy by the collar, lifting him from the ground and tells him very sternly that there's a chance the robots will kill him and his parents. After all, he needs honesty. When Sarah gives her the, "What the hell are you doing?" reprimand, Cameron quickly remembers proper social rituals and asks the young boy, "Would you like a bedtime story?" Yeah, he'd probably like that. Along with being put back on the ground and dry pants now that the ones he's wearing are soaked with urine.

D. Asperger Trait: Needs to be reminded of personal space.

Scenario: John (to Cameron): "When you talk to people, don't stand so close." Of course, there's a practical explanation for this. Cameron (to John) explains why: "I'm assessing the threat level." Well obviously. Only then can she determine if it's time to call nine millimeter.

XII.

Daily Living

No Decorations, Plain Walls and Environment

Constructing buildings, they may do. Decorating buildings, they will never do.

Some Aspergers prefer to live in very plain environments. This means no pictures on the walls, no decorations around the house and in some cases, no furniture other than what is absolutely necessary.

Who knows why the Asperger prefers bare walls to flashy ones.

But the preference for a plain-Jane room will sometimes cause a rift between the Asperger and his extreme home makeover loving neurotypical peers. Co-workers and managers may think the Asperger is going to give two weeks' notice any day after months have gone by and not a picture of a family member or motivational poster has been plastered on his/her desk.

The suggestion of decorations by friends and family will likely be rebuked, unless the decorations have some significance to something the Asperger is interested in such as their collection of poster-sized limited edition postal stamps or pictures of bat species.

Eventually, the Asperger may have to put his/her foot down and explain there will never be a change in décor. This could be done (preferably) directly or passive aggressively.

As a last resort, the Asperger could decorate his home/room with odd or even creepy items to give the home makeover fans a hint.

Some suggestions include weird forms of fetishes. Like clowns. Telling everyone you have a thing for Bozo in drag might quiet some. Alternatively, pictures of the people who are antagonizing the Asperger to decorate may also make a point. Lining the four walls of a room with nothing but photographs of Person X (especially photographs that were taken from a distance without him realizing it) is a surefire way to get Person X off the Asperger's case about making the room look pretty. It will probably get Person X off his case, his phone records and list of people who are willing to invite him over.

In summary, not everybody likes to decorate, especially some Aspergers.

Neurotypicals should realize when it comes to home décor, it's best to keep your opinion and your oil paintings to yourself.

Structure and Routine

If you're looking for a great gift for an Asperger, a day planner in the Christmas stocking may tickle him pink. An hourly planner or a scheduler that allows him to document activities down to the very minute will make him orgasmic. Aspies are known for loving routines and will often adhere to them in a very rigid manner, putting certain activities in very specific time slots.

The Asperger's parents knew they had to keep routines as much as possible or they would experience a temper tantrum or meltdown that caused the emotional trauma to everyone around them the equivalent of an F5 tornado. As adults, these Aspies learn to moderate their needs for intense structure amongst other people—like learning how not to pick up the chair and throw it like an F5 tornado does when learning his lunch break will be changed due to business needs. However, make no mistake, the Aspie will always love structured routines at heart, and will often, even in secrecy, build these routines into their daily lives.

A typical morning routine of an NT from 6:00 a.m. – 7:00 a.m. will include (hopefully) showering, grooming facial and head hair, eating breakfast and (hopefully) brushing the teeth. Contrast this to the extremely structured morning the Asperger may partake in:

6:00 a.m.: Alarm rings. Hit snooze.

6:10 a.m.: Alarm rings. Hit snooze again.

6:20 a.m.: Finally, time to wake up after snoozes twice. Asperger will never snooze once. Or none at all in fear doing so will mess up his entire wakefulness schedule.

6:20 a.m.-6:40 a.m.: Shower. Yes, in 20 minutes when it takes others only five. Wash every body part in the same sequence it's been washed since learning how to do it on their own. Scrub a particular number of times on each part. Don't miss a square inch.

6:40 a.m.: Moisturize. Same rules as the shower for each part and square inch. Left leg always gets moisturizer first.

6:45 a.m.: Pour cereal into bowl.

6:45 a.m.-6:49 a.m.: Pour non-dairy, lactose-free milk into bowl. Cereal needs to sit a few minutes because it doesn't taste right too crunchy. And the gustatory sensory sensitivities can't handle that. Must take first bite before 6:50 a.m. Not because you're in a rush, but because the flakes won't be as crispy, rendering an uneatable bowl of cereal rejected by the gustatory sensory sensitivities.

7:20 a.m.: Brush teeth. Wet toothbrush for five seconds before doing so. Give each tooth five strokes with the toothbrush on all reachable sides.

On any given day, the Asperger will pray there are no interruptions—like a phone call—that will seriously screw up the entire day and a perfectly good bowl of corn flakes.

Camouflaging Asperger's

An Asperger knows how to be a good actor when necessary and will often use imitation to carry out various scenarios in different social settings when it's not as easy to conduct themselves naturally.

Using the appropriate kinds of conversational pieces and physical gestures can be a great way to get through everyday transactions.

After being conditioned to respond in the right manner after so many years, it's all too easy to lie, lie, lie. And based on past experiences, not answering the questions appropriately usually has negative consequences because neurotypicals have a tendency to jump to conclusions instead of using data to drive their decision given the fact they spend so much time socializing at the bar instead of reading about research and studies.

Random question from neurotypical: Do you enjoy socializing with others?

Asperger: Of course, love it! (Thinking: The last time I answered, "no," I got dozens of annoying people who spend too much time talking to other annoying people who fail to understand the happiness that only occurs when I'm with my animals (I own chickens) and when they're with me (I let them sleep in my room. In my bed.). Me and Chicken Little sometimes enjoy snacking on the same foods—the same Grape-Nuts I've been eating as a snack for the last 20 years.

Yeah...it's easy to see why an Asperger has a tendency to not disclose their true selves.

Camouflaging Aspergerness may be easier for girls than boys as some social behaviors are readily seen as normal for girls to do. Like just sitting among other girls and being quiet instead of contributing to the conversation, thus hiding the strange speech style they possess or not revealing the 1,000 facts they've picked up that the other girls aren't likely to be interested in.

This is horrible for girls, as they miss the opportunity to develop the interests and identity they would normally be able to if they didn't have to spend so much time and energy on practicing to smile and answer questions with that upbeat, cheery voice that women in the 1950s were trained to emulate during finishing school lessons.

Not to mention how annoying it is to flip "on" and "off" the different personas used to camouflage the fact they'd rather be discussing politics instead of planning their next appointment for some random female activity that has no logical objective, such as the next nail salon trip.

Practicality

Unless you can offer a good reason for a request, an Asperger isn't likely to look at it as being important.

Aspies are known for their practicality in everything they do and will be sticklers about living this way, even when it's obvious it annoys the heck out of everyone else.

To the Aspie, everything said or done has a purpose—or at least it should have.

The most obvious way this belief is demonstrated is through conversation. While neurotypicals may talk to strengthen a social bond with another, the Asperger is only interested in talking if there's something that needs to be conveyed for a purpose. Office chatter and gossip is likely to annoy them, and they may only speak when asking a question or otherwise trying to get information needed to complete a task.

The same is true for conversations held at home with the family. Discussing finances or plans to visit relatives is important, but not so much how the other spouse's day went.

Obviously, this is a source of frustration for NTs who grow tired of having to think of a logical reason just to convince their AS friend to pay attention to them.

Practicality extends beyond communication and is often the rule of thumb when it comes to regular habits, like dressing, where comfort trumps fashion and tries to trump dress code. Especially when the dress code contains all sorts of unpractical rules like stockings during the summer when it's 101 degrees Fahrenheit outside.

Relationships involving Aspergers may also be viewed in terms of their practicality. At the most extreme, the Asperger husband will view sexual relations as a means to procreate—thus seeing no need for much relations after 2.5 children are created. Similarly, the wife may view him as good for fixing minor repairs around the house, managing the taxes and being in charge of the retirement investing. Or even cooking the family's meals or serving as chauffeur for the children's extracurricular activities. Actually, the wife will view him as pretty much good for everything other than a romantic romp.

The Look—And It's the Only Look

Look through an online publication containing fashion news and trends and you'll often find tags associated with the models wearing the outfits that say, "Get the look," telling the reader the exact brand and style of clothing, the price and even possibly where to order it online. Somewhere in the world of marketing, someone has figured that this will cause everyone to rush out and 1. Buy the hideous looking outfits to keep up with the trends or 2. Some hideous looking person will buy them in hopes it will make them look like a fashion model or 3. Sometimes/usually both.

If one had to tag an Asperger fashion publication for "The Look," it'd be damned easy to coordinate. Along with dressing for comfort and practicality, the Asperger look is one easy to imitate because it often involves the same types of outfits or even the same outfit. Let us examine the top looks in season, every season for the Asperger. Here's how to get "The Look."

The Same Outfit: Not much to say about this one. This Asperger will often wear his favorite pair of jeans and t-shirt everywhere he goes. Or the same pair of jogging/sweatpants. The same sweatshirt. You get the point. This does not mean this Asperger owns only one pair of shirt/jeans. In fact, he could go out and buy a month's worth of the same pair of jeans and the same t-shirt, so he doesn't have to wash often.

The Same Type of Clothing Article: Unlike the same outfit Aspie, this Asperger would never be caught in the same blue t-shirt.

But you will always see them in a t-shirt. Even when it's snowing and negative below outside in February. This Asperger will gravitate toward a certain item and always, always wear it. It could be A-line skirts. Or corduroy pants. This Aspie may have 365 blazers in her closet of assorted colors and diverse materials—green, red, purple, polyester, cotton and denim—and wear a different blazer each day of the week. But rest assured she will always have a blazer on and feel naked without one.

The Same Patterns: An itsy, bitsy, teeny, weenie, yellow, polka-dot bikini. And a polka dot tie. Or a polka dot pair of pants. Or a polka dot shirt. Ditto for stripes, ruffles and other distinctive patterns. Thank goodness the tie-dyed era is no longer in style.

The Same Colors: Some like it in browns. Or greens. Or yellows. Once an Aspie gets turned on to a color, most every outfit they wear will be a variation of that color. The color-coded Aspie is no boring one as there are often dozens of varieties of a color they can pick from. A red-loving Aspie can fill her wardrobe with crimson, auburn, burgundy, maroon, rose, sangria, ruby, chestnut, orange-red, fuchsia and even burnt sienna. Yep, her closet has more variations of one color than a 120-count Crayola crayon box.

The Same Texture: This may be primarily because some textures irritate the sensory sensitivities because they are scratchy, heavy, etc. Some Aspies like the same textures, such as all cotton, polyesters and so forth.

Forgetting What Works

You know the old saying. If you make the same mistake over and over and expect different results, it's called Asperger. Sometimes it's hard for the Asperger to learn from mistakes and some have theorized this may be due to impairments in executive functioning—a fancy psychological term for the brain's ability to plan, initiate and perform activities.

These are generalizations of course and this is not to say that all Aspergers have problems learning from mistakes, especially if those mistakes are paired with strong uncomfortable stimuli, such as a physical or psychological injury or an experience that agitates one of the extremely sensitive sensory sensitivities. Let's say you walk into one popular retail clothing store found at every mall in America that is known for playing music very loudly. You know, the one with all those scandalously racy, controversial-inciting posters of half-naked models plastered on the wall. The one that has gotten store managers cited for obscenity violations because he refused to take them down. Hint, hint, it also carries a perfume baring the same name as the retailer that is equally overwhelming to the senses. After your first experience with hearing this blaring music, regardless of how sexy the barely legally dressed young model is, you may quickly learn it is much easier to shop online from this retailer.

An alternative theory is that some Aspergers are so driven to perfectionism, it makes it difficult to recognize a painful mistake.

On the far end of that spectrum, you have your ASSpergers who refuse to believe there is a mistake to be learned from.

The worst possible thing you could do is start avoiding all the situations where you make mistakes so it's best to have some sort of action plan when redundancy kicks in. A good way to do this is by relying upon one of the strongest Aspie traits—making lists. Lists of everything that did or didn't happen, went right or wrong or blew up—along with the solutions you attempted and whether those worked, as well as some possible way to prevent the mistake in the future. If you are the obsessively organizational Asperger, these lists can be categorized and filed under ideas like events, places, people, etc. For example, under "Mistakes Made When Cooking," you can write brief notes under item #217547 on the list that reads "Burned Food in Microwave Again" that read something similar to, "Stay by microwave, watch and listen for popping to slow for 2-3 seconds. Stop, remove and eat a bag of goodness," vs., "Got distracted and absorbed by the patterns on the feathers of the ducks that fraternize in the neighborhood lake."

So, when that condescending relative, friend or teacher sarcastically says, "Smart people learn from their mistakes, stupid people do not," you can reply that, "Smart people learn from their mistakes, but stupid people don't make lists with nearly half of the instructional value that I make. "

This statement will at least confuse them. It may even serve to educate them.

Eating the Same Foods Everyday

The Asperger child was easy to recognize in the school cafeteria as she always brought the same meal for lunch every day. While other children may have had their parents to blame for this matter ("You eat what we serve you," "That is too expensive.") and often protested, the Asperger child actually enjoyed this. When it came time to barter one's lunch for someone else's, the Asperger never took part in this marketplace. However, no one was ever really interested in exchanging food with him because the meal the Asperger child brought was probably bland and/or really weird anyway.

These Aspergers grew into adults who retained their restrictive food preferences, usually due to their extreme disgust of certain foods, such as tomatoes, the inability to tolerate the texture of many foods or just the plain love of certain types of foods. Tom still brings pasta with marinara sauce daily for lunch, has not strayed in 10 years and would probably have to go on a leave of absence should there be a reason he could not prepare it daily.

This restrictive food fetish comes with its perks. Obviously, there is less planning involved in the process. When she finally arrives at the cash register after standing in line at Howie's Bagels for 10 minutes, the Asperger often finds her everything bagel already made to her liking and wrapped, ready to ring up, provided the workers have spotted her in the back of the line. When seated at restaurants frequented, the Asperger becomes a dignitary, being greeted with elite titles as, "Greek Vegetables?" vs. plain Mr. or Mrs. Eisenhower.

The Aspergers will find their favorite items at the store and often empty the shelves soon after they are stocked, leaving others to wonder why the items are never there even though they've requested the manager to bring them in week after week. Their questions are answered after a careful stakeout reveals a man rolling a cart away with 30 Momma Mia Spinach Lasagnas just moments after they are put in the freezer.

"We switched distributors and they no longer carry the product," is one of the worse phrases the Asperger can hear from the grocer when referring to his favorite food. But all is not lost, as there is opportunity to go to another store where management understands the importance of keeping up the relationship with the right distributors that carry the products.

However, the greatest blow, the final dagger that may leave the Asperger distraught for days, weeks, even months is:

"I'm sorry, sir. The company discontinued the product."

Eating Routines and Food Presentation Preferences

Along with eating the same foods every day, Aspergers like to stick to eating routines and reliable ways of having their food presented on the plate. That whole "the kid likes it sliced in triangles and not rectangles" sandwich thing is no joke for the Asperger. They may even eat in a particular order, such as green vegetables first, eat clockwise or counterclockwise, no mixing of side dishes, the ridiculous list goes on and on.

This may make for a challenging experience at restaurants when someone is not as in tuned to the Asperger's particular eating preferences. If the Asperger is used to his favorite dish with finely chopped cucumbers and it is brought out in big chunks the chef has committed a sin worthy of three Hail Marys. An innocent waiter may even try to convince the Asperger the dish isn't supposed to be different than what he received, but the Asperger is no fool! He knows the waiter is trying to pull one over on him in an attempt to get him to shut his mouth and tip well. The Asperger becomes even more determined to pursue the case of why the dish looks, smells and tastes differently than it did the last 200 times.

"More cornstarch?"

"We don't use cornstarch. We use potato flour."

"Different brand of rice?"

"We've been using the same rice for the past decade."

"Different area of the farm the cabbage was picked from?"

"How the #$@! would I know?"

Much ado will take place that involves supervisors, managers and prime ministers if they can take a phone call. Dozens of trips to the kitchen and several conversations with the manager will result in the Asperger finally getting the meal presented in the way he likes—or the meal being dumped on his head.

Dressing for Comfort and Practicality

Clothes may make the neurotypical man or woman, but they will never make the Asperger.

Aspergers generally have no use for the latest fashions and would prefer to wear clothing for comfort and practical purposes. Much to the disappointment of the Asperger's friends and family, the Asperger will continue to dress him or herself for these comfort and practical purposes even after constant reprimands, lessons and downright rude comments made to motivate them to change.

An Asperger female may find herself at greater risk, as the neurotypical female species places more importance on clothing and style. As one male once stated, "A man would not think twice about wearing the same thing twice in a week. A girl would think it was horrible to wear the same thing twice in a month." So, when an Asperger girl wears her favorite pair of pumps with every outfit—including her jogging pants—nasty words are going to fly. Ditto for untucked shirts, colors that don't match, clothing with rips and tears or that same pair of black pants that has been washed so many times, it is now gray.

Many helpful hints will be passed on to the Asperger. "Look through the latest fashion catalogues and copy your wardrobe like the models." Some will comply, with graciousness or annoyance.

A good way for the not-so-compliant Asperger to cease these ~~nagging~~ helpful hints is to simply follow the advice given. A smart

Asperger would go out and find a fashion magazine and plan their wardrobe exactly after the models. The best brand to model after is Victoria's Secret, especially for men. Once an Asperger's parents see their son in pink wings and a push-up, they might back off and make a deal that you only have to be mindful of clothing for a job interview or work itself—not going to the friggin' grocery store.

Adult costume stores are also good places for ideas. You could put together a nice outfit based upon dozens of characters, from "Naughty Nurse" to "Temptress Teacher."

By utilizing these solutions, Aspergers can ensure they always look trendy, pleasing everyone in their lives who are concerned with their normality and ability to blend with neurotypicals. Victoria's Secret never carries yesterday's fashions. And sex shop costumes might be very open and revealing in various places, thus preventing any tight feelings on the skin for those with sensory sensitivity issues. If there are any objections, remind those around you you're simply following their advice. And that the outfit you're wearing matches, which is by far the most important thing.

XIII.

Identity

Privacy

For some reason, many Aspies value their privacy as much as Internet sites value cookies to take away that privacy. Or grocery stores valuing tracking your purchases and pretending to give you discounts on the same item they've overcharged for weeks. Or people who like to be nosy and look right into someone's front yard by entering their address in Google Maps. You get the picture.

While many Aspergers will tell you how important their privacy is to them, some can't exactly pinpoint why. Maybe it's because privacy is sometimes related to the very much valued solitude and—to the Asperger—the two are essentially the same.

Sometimes private matters, such as secrets, personal thoughts and all other bits of information routinely shared by reality TV stars to millions of people, are often shared with smaller groups of people that neurotypicals trust in social settings. If the typical Aspie doesn't like a lot of socializing, his radar of discomfort may go off because giving up privacy is something associated with another task he doesn't like very much.

When interacting with people in the world, sharing is almost inevitable and most people you interact with will eventually get to know all sorts of juicy information about you like age and background, skills sets, salary range and even diet. Most Aspergers have had more than their share of forced interaction with people, through school work and even growing up in a home that could rival *The Brady Bunch* in siblings. All this excessive exposure to other people may have backfired.

Unfortunately, there isn't a good explanation for the freakishness level of privacy Aspies need.

Until one is created, keep making up those strange usernames online. And keeping the door to your office closed. And maintaining an unpublished phone number. And using the picture of your cat in place of a photo on online dating websites. And keeping who you do and don't date a secret from co-workers, family and even the cat.

Maybe you'll find a Facebook group page where you can discuss the issue with other Aspies until someone else finds a solution.

Nah, you probably won't be able to find it because the Asperger who created it was too stringent with the public settings.

Shame from ASSpergers

While most of the time, Aspies have nothing but a sense of pride in their culture, there are times when the worst of them gets to them. Usually, Aspergerness can be characterized as positive traits with a few minor social hang-ups. Occasionally, an Asperger makes the news, whether that'd be the neighborhood gossip circle or *The New York Times*, for doing something really, really bad. Or using the term Asperger to describe really, really inappropriate social behavior.

This person becomes known to neurotypicals and other Aspies as the ASSperger.

Aspies have enough to worry about, many fearing the consequences and even discrimination that may surface if they reveal who they are (the ones who are actually able to hide it). And there's no worse time to come out of the Aspie closet than when George X, John Y and Cindy Z have made CNN that week for hacking, displaying bad manners or being a bitch.

In a way, this shame that Aspies feel is no different from what many other people who belong to a particular group such as a town, religious sect or club feel when someone from that group does something notorious. Somewhere, in a small town hidden in a remote area of Georgia, there are people turning on the news at any given moment, saying things like, "Man, why did it have to be a six-fingered, attached ear-lobed, blue-haired, half-android, half-human guy who did that? As if we don't have enough stereo-types about us!"

There's really nothing you can do about it.

Except wait a couple of weeks after the ASSperger's fame gained from his temper outburst in Times Square is replaced with headlines about the four-fingered, half-human, half-android man streaking in public to open up and come out about your Asperger's to people who know you shouldn't lump all Aspies and half-human, half-android people into one category.

Androgyny

Having the best of both worlds is great, and many Aspies have the ability to understand both sexes from a cultural point of view because they are natural androgynes.

Instead of exhibiting extreme traditional male or female traits, Asperger males and females will often find their personalities planting firmly in the middle, while at the same time freely dabbling in either gender role as they desire. They may dress, behave and take on roles in society that are sometimes associated with the opposite gender without giving it a second thought.

Whatever traits these Aspies possess, there is one thing they all have in common: they view themselves as human before a man or a woman. And don't expect them to change by suggesting they model and emulate the other girls and boys.

Androgyny has thrived in pop culture, with some very famous performers like David Bowie and Annie Lennox being given the designation by pop culture experts. Some have attributed the rise in '90s "pretty boy bands" like Backstreet Boys, New Kids on the Block, NSYNC and Take That to an even further push toward redefining what is considered the male sex symbol. Movies now depict very feminine-looking females portraying male roles in hard-core action films. Fashion designers are making more of their garments "gender neutral," and we are seeing more models strut the catwalks in jackets, pants and other attire in colors, shades and styles that can be envisioned on any sex. And who doesn't love guyliner?

Okay, not everyone. But any male who does sure knows how to push a gender boundary.

Experts in the field of androgyny, like psychologist Sandra Bem, describe people with it as being more flexible and mentally healthy than overly feminine or masculine individuals. Some have even linked the rise in androgyny to a society where gains are made economically and socially, such as women delaying childbirth and becoming more educated and independent.

With so many positives for both Aspergers and NTs, the androgynous perspective should only be embraced further. Even if it means putting up with a reunion of New Kids on the Block.

If They Knew What They Want

Neurotypicals complaining about Aspergers not being able to relate to them should stop for a minute and consider this: Sometimes the Asperger is so busy trying to figure out what he wants, he doesn't have any room left to attend to their needs. And figuring out what he wants could take forever.

Because of their impaired theory of mind (fancy term coined by neuro-psychy people studying why Aspergers do so many weird things), Aspergers find it hard to guess and predict the thoughts, motivations, intentions and feelings of others. Because of his impaired theory of mind, an Asperger also finds it hard to guess and predict the thoughts, motivations, intentions and feelings of himself. In a strange twist of neural wiring, Aspies sometimes can't figure out if or why they want something or what motivates them and why they do and don't do something in particular.

Which makes The Bangles' song from the '80s, "If She Knew What She Wants," (originally written and sung by Jules Shear) the perfect anthem for them.

One good illustration of this in pop culture is an episode from the Fox television series *Family Guy* where the Griffin son Chris is trying to socialize by joining the Republican Party club at his school. A young girl in the club tries to convince him to do her a favor and entices him with the reward of showing him her bare chest.

"Do I want that (to see her bare chest)?" Chris asks.

"Yes, you do," the girl replies.

Darn that impaired theory of mind. It may make an Asperger turn down a free DVD from Girls Gone Wild.

Figuring out what they want takes more time for an Asperger than a neurotypical, as there is usually a lot of deliberation, weighing both sides, researching options and good old-fashioned time spent alone holed up in a room.

One of the worst things a neurotypical can do at this point is flat out tell the Asperger what she wants. There is an enormous chance of the Asperger being misunderstood and having words put in her mouth—something she definitely knows she doesn't want.

The A-word

Just like many other groups or cultures in society, Aspergers have playfully given themselves nicknames. The most common and universally accepted nickname is Aspie—which is useful for not only generating discussion either in person or online about the topic, but also serves as something that helps to identify each other among the sea of neurotypicals. You could call it an antenna that helps the Asperger's radar (the Aspergerdar), pick up on any Aspie within thousands of miles. Or at least within a few feet of comfortable "personal spaces" during conversation.

Hearing the word Aspie in a conversation, you—because you are an Asperger—are tempted to interrupt. You may be so overwhelmed with excitement, the social rules you usually follow are thrown out the window as you quickly jump in to conduct a conversation in a completely different language than the neurotypicals around you. For the anxious that are forced to walk gingerly in the regular NT culture, it can bring a sigh of relief now that you are able to carry out a social interaction with someone usually much more rational and logical. And for the Asperger snobs not yet attached to someone, this signals the sign of a potential mate. Some animals sing and whistle. Some dance and show off their feathers. And some casually drop the word Aspie while talking too much about their collection of 500 designer ties they never wear and instantly woo over the female.

The word Asperger can be used by a variety of people and not necessarily in a good way. It could be coming from an Aspie ally who wants to educate people about all the wonderful points about them. Or it could be from a complete moron who makes up inaccurate facts about their intelligence, predisposition towards behaviors or ability to match their socks in the morning.

Using the word Aspie is a privilege and reserved only for those who truly understand the culture and possess positive feelings about it. Aspergers use it. But so do all of their friends, family, smart experts and neurotypicals who have a healthy respect for their differences.

An outsider simply calling an Asperger the A-word is not likely to cause offense, create lawsuits citing pain and suffering or even elicit a few fighting words normally reserved between drunks at the bar at 3:00 a.m. However, using the A-word in a derogatory manner, when you are not qualified to do so or in a way that makes you look both not qualified and stupid (e.g. Aspies usually don't have a life or friends. That Aspie man could not possibly have a girlfriend.) is likely to result in swift punishment from one or more members from the community, depending on the environment or how many people are logged in the forum and in the mood for some good online ass-kicking.

Printed in Great Britain
by Amazon

39444871R00126